Swadisht Subzian

TARLA DALAL
India's #1 Cookery Author

SANJAY & CO.
BOMBAY

Third Printing : 2005

Copyright © Sanjay & Co.

ISBN : 81-86469-79-6

Price Rs. 189/-

Published & Distributed by :

SANJAY & COMPANY

353/A-1, Shah & Nahar Industrial Estate, Dhanraj Mill Compound,
Lower Parel (W), Mumbai - 400 013. INDIA.
Tel. : (91-22) 2496 8068 ● Fax : (91-22) 2496 5876 ● E-mail : sanjay@tarladalal.com

Recipe Research,	**Photography**
Production Design &	VINAY MAHIDHAR
Food Styling	DARSHAN GURAV
PINKY DIXIT	
PRADNYA SUNDARARAJ	

Printed by	**Designed by**
JUPITER PRINTS, Mumbai	S. KISHOR

BULK PURCHASES

Tarla Dalal Cookbooks are ideal gifts. If you are interested in buying
more than 500 assorted copies of Tarla Dalal Cookbooks at special prices,
please contact us at 91-22-2496 8068 or email : sanjay@tarladalal.com

Introduction

Indian cuisine, like Indian geography, culture and climate is rich and diverse. In fact, the finest of India's cuisines is as rich and diverse as it's civilisation. This holds true for the art of preparing vegetables in India. The traditional Indian 'subzian' and their cooking styles too vary from region to region and season to season. Preparing 'subzis' is an art form that has been passed on through generations purely by word of mouth, mother to daughter or daughter-in-law.

The many regional cuisines are a result of the variety of agricultural produce, weather conditions and spices available in different regions of India, which in turn determine their own way of cooking.

The range of 'subzian' assumes astonishing proportions when one takes into account the seasonal and regional variations. Vegetables commonly available all season are potatoes, onions, green peppers (capsicum), tomatoes, and various kinds of beans including green beans, chana, kidney beans and others. These form a part of the every-day fare served with meals. They are served with the main dish of *dal* or cereal. The style of cooking vegetables depends on the main dish or cereal with which they are served.

Very often the taste, colour, texture and appearance of the same *subzi* changes from state to state. The essence of Indian cooking revolves around the use of spices. Spices, used to enhance the flavour of the *subzi*, serve both as appetizers and digestives and are a fundamental part of food preparation. Correct use and blending of the aromatic spices is crucial to the proper preparation of Indian subzian. Even oil is an important part of cooking, whether it's mustard oil in the North or coconut oil in the South, each section of the country has its preferences. Milk products like *ghee, curds* and *paneer* too form a part of the main ingredients of Indian cooking. The same vegetable like aloo can be cooked in ghee and tomato or in *dahi*, and will result in two different and delicious *subzian*.

Across regions, our *subzian* can be subtly spiced or chilli-hot, succulent vegetarian, pungent, savoury or cloyingly sweet, simply baked or simmered in rich sauces of curd and coconut.

Let's try our hands at re-inventing Indian vegetable dishes from different regions and be a part of the " *winsome food experience.*"

Regards,

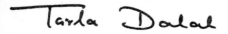

Index

RAJASTHANI

HYDERABADI

SINDHI

SOUTH INDIAN

MAHARASHTRIAN

ROTIS

NORTH INDIAN

The northern region of India stretches from the valley-filled Kashmir to the vast field-lands of Punjab and across Bihar and Uttar Pradesh.

A typical North Indian meal consists of *chapatis* or *rotis* (unleavened bread baked on a *tawa*) or *parathas* (unleavened bread fried on a *tawa*), rice and an assortment of assessories like *dals*, subzian, curries, curd, *chutney*, and pickles. The dishes are rich and delicate, with incredible, bold flavours.

This section showcases vegetables from various northern parts of India like Kashmir, U.P. and Bihar. The cuisines of these regions are related by similar usage of ingredients like aniseed (*saunf*), ginger and dry red chillies. The generous use of cream for the gravies of the vegetables, to impart a rich texture and consistency, is also a common feature in these regions.

Though the ingredients used are similar, each region has its own distinct flavours due to the difference in the blend of spices and flavourings. While the Kashmiri cuisine is a blend of its major produce, which includes red chillies, fruits, nuts, saffron and rajma, the cuisines of U P and Bihar have a strong influence of the Eastern regions of Bengal and Assam.

I have included traditional specialties like the Rajma Saagwala and Nimona along with restaurant favourites like the Hariyali Cheese Kofta and Dum Aloo Benarasi. The very subtly flavoured Jahtpat Subzi serves as a good example for a quick whip up with a delicate blend of spices.

Rajma Saagwala

Picture on facing page

A nutritious protein and fibre rich dish that's delicately flavoured. Amaranth (chawli leaves) can be substituted with other greens like spinach or fenugreek.

❧ **Prep. time : 15 mins.** ❧ **Cooking time : 20 mins.** ❧ **Serves 4.**

½ cup rajma (kidney beans),
soaked, cooked and drained

3 cups amaranth leaves (chawli), chopped

½ teaspoon cumin seeds (jeera)

2 to 3 green chillies, chopped

1 teaspoon ginger, chopped

1 teaspoon garlic, chopped

½ cup onions, chopped

¼ teaspoon turmeric powder (haldi)

¼ teaspoon sugar (optional)

¼ cup cream

1½ teaspoons oil

salt to taste

1. Heat the oil and add the cumin seeds. When they crackle, add the green chillies, ginger, garlic and onions and sauté for 4 to 5 minutes.
2. Add the amaranth leaves, rajma, turmeric powder and salt and bring to a boil.
3. Add the cream and sugar and simmer for another 5 to 7 minutes.

Serve hot with parathas.

Top: Makhani Roti, page 110
Bottom: Rajma Saagwala, recipe above

Paneer and Corn Curry

Filling and flavourful. This recipe is best made with yellow (sweet) corn, although tender white corn kernels can also be used instead.

✍ Prep. time : 30 mins. ✍ Cooking time : 30 mins. ✍ Serves 4.

1 cup paneer (cottage cheese),
cut into 25 mm. (1") cubes

1 cup sweet corn kernels, boiled

½ cup onions, puréed

1 bay leaf

25 mm. (1") stick cinnamon (dalchini)

2 cloves (laung)

1 teaspoon chilli powder

4 tomatoes, blanched, peeled and puréed

½ cup curds, beaten

2 tablespoons cream

1 teaspoon sugar

½ teaspoon garam masala

2 tablespoons oil

salt to taste

✍ For the paste

1 tablespoon broken cashewnuts

1 tablespoon poppy seeds (khus-khus)

2 cloves garlic

12 mm. (½") piece ginger

3 tablespoons warm milk

✍ For the garnish

chopped coriander

✍ For the paste

1. Soak the cashewnuts and poppy seeds in warm milk for 20 to 30 minutes.
2. Add the garlic and ginger and grind to a smooth paste. Keep aside.

✍ How to proceed

1. Heat the oil in a pan, add the onions, bay leaf, cinnamon and cloves and sauté till the onions turn golden brown in colour.
2. Add the chilli powder, ground paste and tomatoes and simmer for 3 to 4 minutes.
3. Add the curds, cream, sugar, garam masala and salt and simmer till the gravy thickens and the oil separates from the masala.
4. Add some water to thin down the consistency of the gravy if required. Add the paneer and corn and mix well.

Serve hot garnished with the coriander.

Karela Mussalam

Deep fried strips of bitter gourd in a tangy onion-tomato gravy. I am sure after savouring this dish, you will strike off bitter gourds from your 'do not like' list. Remember to choose slim green bitter gourds with soft flesh and less seeds for best results.

❧ **Prep. time : 45 mins.** ❧ **Cooking time : 45 mins.** ❧ **Serves 4.**

2 cups (250 grams) karela (bitter gourd)
½ teaspoon cumin seeds (jeera)
1 cup onions, finely chopped
1 teaspoon ginger-garlic paste
1 teaspoon chilli powder
2 teaspoons coriander seed (dhania) powder
¼ teaspoon turmeric powder (haldi)
1½ cups tomatoes, chopped
3 tablespoons cream
2 tablespoons tomato purée
½ teaspoon sugar
1 tablespoon oil
salt to taste

❧ **Other ingredients**
oil for deep frying

1. Peel and cut the karela into 50 mm. (2") pieces. Deseed and cut it into thin strips. Sprinkle salt over the karela strips and keep aside for 40 to 45 minutes.
2. Wash and drain the karela. Dry on an absorbent towel.
3. Deep fry the karela strips in hot oil over a medium flame till they are golden brown. Drain on absorbent paper and keep aside.
4. Heat the oil and add the cumin seeds. When they crackle, add the onions and sauté till they are golden brown.
5. Add the ginger-garlic paste, chilli powder, coriander seed powder, turmeric powder and 1 cup of water and simmer for 4 to 5 minutes.
6. Add the tomatoes and cook till the oil separates from the gravy.
7. Add the cream and tomato purée and mix well.
8. Add the karela, sugar and salt and mix well.
9. Simmer for 3 to 4 minutes and serve hot.

Palak Mutter

Simple, subtle and superb! An aromatic Kashmiri vegetable flavoured with an unusual combination of spices.

Prep. time : 10 mins. Cooking time : 20 mins. Serves 4.

5 cups spinach (palak), finely chopped
1 cup green peas, boiled
2 cloves (laung)
25 mm. (1") stick cinnamon (dalchini)
¼ teaspoon asafoetida (hing)
1 teaspoon chilli powder
¼ teaspoon turmeric powder (haldi)
¼ teaspoon ginger powder (soonth)
½ cup milk
2 teaspoons oil
salt to taste

1. Heat the oil, add the cloves, cinnamon and asafoetida.
2. Add the spinach and peas along with ½ cup of water and bring it to a boil.
3. Simmer for 10 to 12 minutes till almost all the water evaporates.
4. Add the chilli powder, turmeric powder, ginger powder, milk and salt and mix well.
5. Bring it to a boil and serve immediately.

Dum Aloo Banarasi

Dum means cooking in steam. Dum cooking brings the oil or ghee, used for the preparation, to the top of the dish thus improving its appearance. This Dum Aloo preparation uses baby potatoes which are easier to cook. You may however, use medium sized potatoes, each cut into 2, if you do not find baby potatoes.

ಬ **Prep. time : 10 mins.** ಬ **Cooking time : 20 mins.** ಬ **Serves 4.**

12 to 15 baby potatoes
oil for deep frying

ಬ For the gravy

2 cups tomatoes, roughly chopped
3 cloves garlic
25 mm. (1") piece ginger
8 dry Kashmiri chillies
2 tablespoons cashewnuts, broken
1 teaspoon cumin seeds (jeera)
1 teaspoon fennel seeds (saunf)
2½ cups water

ಬ Other ingredients

8 green cardamoms (elaichi)
1 tablespoon kasuri methi
(dried fenugreek seeds), roasted
1 tablespoon honey
¼ cup fresh cream
1 tablespoon chopped coriander
2 teaspoons butter
1 teaspoon oil
salt to taste

1. Wash and dry the baby potatoes. Pierce each potato all around with a fork and deep fry in hot oil, with the skin on, till the potatoes are cooked.
2. Drain on absorbent paper and keep aside.

ಬ For the gravy

1. Combine all the ingredients together and simmer over a medium flame till the tomatoes are cooked.
2. Cool the mixture and purée in a blender to make a smooth paste.

ಬ How to proceed

1. Heat the butter and oil in a pan, add the cardamom and gravy paste and allow it to come to a boil. Simmer till the oil separates form the gravy.
2. Add the potatoes, kasuri methi, honey and salt and simmer for some more time.
3. Add the cream and coriander and serve hot.

Saunfwale Aloo Baingan

Brinjal and potato make an interesting combination as they complement each other in taste as well in texture. A hint of fennel adds an authentic North Indian touch to this subzi. Serve it with dal, chawal and phulkas to make a complete meal.

Prep. time : 15 mins. Cooking time : 20 mins. Serves 4.

1 cup potatoes, peeled and thickly sliced
1 cup brinjal, thickly sliced
½ teaspoon cumin seeds (jeera)
½ cup onions, thickly sliced
1 teaspoon ginger, grated
1 teaspoon garlic, grated
¼ teaspoon turmeric powder (haldi)
¾ teaspoon chilli powder
1 tablespoon oil
salt to taste

To be roasted and ground
1 tablespoon whole coriander (dhania) seeds
1 tablespoon fennel seeds (saunf)

For the garnish
2 tablespoons chopped coriander

1. Heat the oil and add the cumin seeds.
2. When they crackle, add the onions and sauté for 3 to 5 minutes.
3. Add the potatoes, salt and ¼ cup of water. Cover and cook over a slow flame till the potatoes are half cooked. Add the ginger and garlic and mix well.
4. Add the brinjal and cover and cook for another 7 to 10 minutes over a slow flame till the brinjal is almost cooked.
5. Add the turmeric powder, chilli powder and coriander and fennel seed powder and mix well. Cover and cook for 3 to 4 minutes, till the masalas are cooked.

Serve hot garnished with the coriander.

Nimona

The cuisine of any region is incomplete unless it includes a homemakers contribution. Nimona is one such example from Lucknow, the capital of Avadh. A strictly home-fare dish, this delectable preparation is made with green peas puréed with tomatoes to make a dal like gravy.

❧ **Prep. time : 15 mins.** ❧ **Cooking time : 25 mins.** ❧ **Serves 4.**

1 cup green peas, boiled
1 cup potatoes, boiled and cubed
½ teaspoon cumin seeds (jeera)
½ cup onions, sliced
1 bay leaf
1 black cardamom
½ teaspoon garlic, grated
1 teaspoon ginger, grated
2 teaspoons coriander seed (dhania) powder
1 teaspoon chilli powder
¼ teaspoon turmeric powder (haldi)
½ cup puréed tomatoes
½ teaspoon garam masala
1 tablespoon oil
salt to taste

1. Purée the green peas in a blender using a little water and keep aside.
2. Heat the oil in a non-stick pan and add the cumin seeds, onions, bay leaf and cardamom and sauté over a slow flame till the onions turn golden brown.
3. Add the garlic and ginger and sauté for 2 to 3 more minutes.
4. Add the coriander seed powder, chilli powder, turmeric powder and puréed tomatoes and cook till the oil separates from the gravy.
5. Add the green pea purée and sauté for 2 to 3 minutes till the mixture leaves the sides of the pan.
6. Add the potatoes, salt and 1½ cups of water and mix well.
7. Bring to a boil and simmer till the gravy thickens.

Serve hot sprinkled with the garam masala.

Kathal Ki Subzi

This recipe makes use of raw jackfruit which absorbs all the flavours easily because of its subtle flavour. Unlike ripened jackfruit, this is a delightful harmony of flavour and textures. Cut raw jackfruit with well oiled hands as it secretes a sap which does not wash off easily.

❧ **Prep. time : 15 mins.** ❧ **Cooking time : 20 mins.** ❧ **Serves 4.**

2 cups raw jackfruit (kathal), diced
¼ teaspoon turmeric powder (haldi)
25 mm. (1") stick cinnamon (dalchini)
4 to 5 cloves (laung)
3 bay leaves
1 cup onions, sliced
1 tablespoon ginger, chopped
1 tablespoon garlic, chopped
1 cup tomatoes, chopped
2 teaspoons coriander seed (dhania) powder
1 teaspoon cumin seed (jeera) powder
2 teaspoons chilli powder
3 tablespoons oil
salt to taste

❧ **For the garnish**
¼ cup chopped coriander

1. In a bowl, mix together the jackfruit, turmeric, salt and 1 tablespoon of oil. Keep aside for 10 to 15 minutes.
2. In a pressure cooker, add the remaining 2 tablespoons of oil, cinnamon, cloves and bay leaves and sauté for a few seconds.
3. Add the onions, ginger and garlic and cook till onions are lightly browned.
4. Add the tomatoes, coriander seed powder, cumin seed powder and chilli powder and cook till the oil is released from the tomato mixture.
5. Add the marinated jackfruit and sauté for 4 to 5 minutes.
6. Add 1½ cups of water and pressure cook for 2 whistles over a medium flame.
7. Open the cooker and dry out liquid if there is any.
8. Garnish with the coriander and serve hot.

Jhatpat Subzi

Picture on page 31

A colourful medley of vegetables lightly sautéed make this delicious dish.

ఐ Prep. time : a few minutes ఐ Cooking time : 10 mins. ఐ Serves 4.

1 cup baby corn, boiled and sliced
1 cup paneer (cottage cheese), diced
1 cup capsicum (all 3 colours), cubed
1 teaspoon cumin seeds (jeera)
1 teaspoon green chilli-ginger paste
1 tablespoon oil
salt to taste

ఐ Other ingredients
oil for deep frying

1. Deep fry the paneer in hot oil until golden in colour. Drain on absorbent paper and keep aside.
2. Heat the oil in a non-stick pan, add the cumin seeds and allow them to crackle.
3. Add the ginger-green chilli paste and the capsicum and sauté for a few minutes till the capsicum is a little tender.
4. Add the baby corn, paneer, salt and 1 to 2 tablespoons of water and cover and cook over a slow flame for 2 minutes.

Serve hot.

Saagwala Cheese Kofta

A tasty, simple recipe of cheese koftas tossed in a flavourful spinach-fenugreek gravy. Add the koftas to the gravy just before serving, as they are soft and crumbly and cannot be simmered in the gravy for a long time.

Prep. time : 15 mins. Cooking time : 30 mins. Serves 4.

For the cheese koftas
½ cup grated cheese
½ cup potatoes, boiled and grated
1 tablespoon raisins (kismis)
1 tablespoon cornflour
1 green chilli, finely chopped
salt to taste

For the green gravy
3 cups chopped spinach (palak), blanched
1 cup fenugreek (methi) leaves, blanched
1 teaspoon cumin seeds (jeera)
1 cup onions, puréed
2 teaspoons ginger-garlic paste
1 green chilli, finely chopped
½ teaspoon kasuri methi (dried fenugreek leaves)
¼ teaspoon turmeric powder (haldi)
4 tablespoons cream
½ teaspoon garam masala
1 tablespoon oil
salt to taste

Other ingredients
oil for deep frying

Top: Lachcha Parathas, page 121
Bottom: Mutter Paneer Butter Masala, page 27

∞ **For the cheese koftas**

1. Combine all the ingredients and mix well.
2. Divide the mixture into 8 equal portions and shape into rounds.
3. Deep fry in hot oil till they are golden brown. Drain on absorbent paper and keep aside.

∞ **For the green gravy**

1. Combine the blanched spinach and fenugreek leaves in a blender and purée to a smooth paste.
2. Heat the oil in a pan and add the cumin seeds.
3. When the seeds crackle, add the puréed onions and sauté till the onions turn golden brown.
4. Add the ginger-garlic paste and green chilli and sauté for 2 to 3 minutes.
5. Add the kasuri methi and turmeric powder and mix well.
6. Add the spinach-fenugreek purée, cream, garam masala, salt with ½ cup of water and bring to a boil.

∞ **How to proceed**

Add the prepared koftas to the hot gravy and serve immediately.

Handy tip : Dip the blanched palak and methi in cold water after blanching. This will help the greens to retain a bright green colour by arresting any further cooking.

PUNJABI

For the Punjabis, *rotis* and *lassi* give them the vigour and energy they are noted for. A typical Punjabi meal consists of roti/parathas/naan/kulcha served with *dal*, vegetable curries, *raita* (spicy yogurt), a cup of rice and pickles. The Punjabis also place a lot of stress on the ginger, garlic, onion and tomato combinations.

The important ingredients in cooking the different dishes are garam masala (a mixture of ground spices available in any Indian Store) and other spices such as cumin, cloves and cinnamon sticks. Alongwith vegetables, paneer also adds more variety to their cooking. Prepared in myriad ways, added to a simple gravy it is eaten as often as vegetables.

Altogether the northern part is famous for its tongue tickling Mughlai dishes. Try some of these sumptuous ways to add more variety to your culinary repertoire.

Mushroom Mutter Makhani

Hearty chunks of mushrooms and green peas replace paneer in this famous Punjabi recipe. You can choose any combination of vegetables to add to this rich tomato based makhani gravy. Serve with naans or parathas to make it a completely gratifying meal.

☊ **Prep. time : 10 mins.** ☊ **Cooking time : 20 mins.** ☊ **Serves 4.**

2 cups mushrooms,
quartered and blanched

1 cup green peas, boiled

½ teaspoon cumin seeds (jeera)

½ cup onions, chopped

1 teaspoon chilli powder

1 teaspoon coriander seed (dhania) powder

a pinch turmeric powder (haldi)

2 tablespoons cream

¼ teaspoon garam masala

1 teaspoon sugar

¼ teaspoon kasuri methi
(dried fenugreek leaves)

2 tablespoons oil

salt to taste

☊ **For the paste**

1½ cups tomatoes, finely chopped

½ cup onions, chopped

2 large cloves garlic

25 mm. (1") piece ginger, chopped

1 tablespoon cashewnuts, broken

☊ **For the garnish**

1 tablespoon chopped coriander

☊ For the paste

1. Combine all the ingredients in a pan with ¼ cup of water and cook till the tomatoes and onions soften.
2. Cool and purée the mixture in a blender to make a paste.
3. Strain the paste and keep aside.

☊ How to proceed

1. Heat the oil and add the cumin seeds.
2. When they crackle, add the onions and sauté for a few minutes.
3. Add the strained paste, chilli powder, coriander seed powder and turmeric powder and simmer for 4 to 5 minutes.
4. Add the cream, garam masala, sugar and kasuri methi with ¼ cup of water and simmer for another 3 to 4 minutes.
5. Add the salt, mushrooms and peas and bring it to a boil.

Serve hot, garnished with the coriander.

Paneer Makhmali

Paneer pieces marinated in an aromatic mint, coriander and cashew paste tossed in buttered onions. This is a very sociable dish if put in the center of the table where people can help themselves with toothpicks. It can also be served as a side dish.

৯৩ **Prep. time : 20 mins.** ৯৩ **Cooking time : 10 mins.** ৯৩ **Serves 4.**

3 cups paneer (cottage cheese), cubed
1 cup onions, sliced
¼ cup milk
1½ teaspoons garam masala
1 tablespoon butter
1 teaspoon oil

৯৩ **To be ground into a thick paste**
2 cups chopped coriander
½ cup mint, chopped
2 to 3 green chillies
25 mm. (1") piece ginger
¼ cup cashewnuts, broken
¼ cup fresh curds
juice of 1 lemon
salt to taste

1. Pierce the paneer pieces with a fork and marinate them in the ground paste for at least 15 minutes.
2. Heat the butter and oil in a pan and sauté the onions till they are translucent.
3. Add the marinated paneer and sauté for 5 to 7 minutes.
4. Add the milk and simmer till the milk evaporates.
5. Sprinkle with the garam masala and serve immediately.

Tandoori Gobi

Succulent pieces of cauliflower marinated in tandoori spices. You can marinate chunks of paneer, mushrooms, or even boiled potatoes to make interesting variations. Serve these with toothpicks to make a conversation starter or with rotis or parathas to make a quick working lunch.

𝕤 **Prep. time : 20 mins.** 𝕤 **Cooking time : 20 mins.** 𝕤 **Serves 4.**

2 cups cauliflower florets, parboiled
½ teaspoon cumin seeds (jeera)
1 cup onions, sliced
1 cup capsicum, sliced
salt to taste
1 teaspoon oil

𝕤 **To be mixed into a marinade**
½ cup curds, beaten
1 teaspoon Bengal gram flour (besan)
1 teaspoon ginger paste
2 teaspoons garlic paste
1 teaspoon chilli powder
½ teaspoon kasoori methi (dried fenugreek leaves)
salt to taste

𝕤 **For the garnish**
1 tablespoon chopped coriander

1. Marinate the cauliflower florets in the prepared marinade for approximately 15 minutes.
2. Heat the oil and add the cumin seeds. When they crackle, add the onions and capsicum and sauté till they are translucent.
3. Add the cauliflower along with the marinade and sauté for 10 to 12 minutes till the cauliflower is cooked.
4. Adjust the salt and serve hot, garnished with the coriander.

Mutter Paneer Butter Masala

Picture on page 21

As the name suggests, this dish is very rich. The soft paneer chunks dunked in a rich tomato based gravy is a must for all those who love paneer.

❧ **Prep. time : 15 mins.** ❧ **Cooking time : 20 mins.** ❧ **Serves 4.**

2½ cups paneer (cottage cheese), cut into cubes

1 teaspoon fenugreek (methi) seeds

¼ cup green peas, boiled

¼ cup onions, diced

2 tablespoons butter

❧ **To be ground to a paste**

1 cup onions, chopped

25 mm. (1") piece ginger

6 to 7 cloves garlic

2 tablespoons broken cashewnuts

❧ **Other ingredients**

1 teaspoon chilli powder

2 cups fresh tomato purée

1 teaspoon cumin seed (jeera) powder

½ teaspoon garam masala

1 tablespoon honey

¼ cup milk

¼ cup cream

1 tablespoon oil

salt to taste

1. Heat the oil in a pan, add the ground paste and cook till it is light brown in colour.
2. Add the chilli powder and tomato purée and cook for a few minutes.
3. Add the cumin seed powder, garam masala and ½ cup of water and cook for some time till the oil separates from the masala. Keep aside.
4. In another pan, melt the butter, add the fenugreek seeds and onions and cook till the onions are lightly browned.
5. Add this to the tomato gravy, along with the peas, honey, milk, cream, paneer and salt and allow it to come to a boil.

Serve hot with rotis or parathas.

Handy tip : Approximately 4 large tomatoes yield 2 cups tomato purée.

Aloo Mutter

A quick and delicious way to make the all time favourite Aloo Mutter. The potato and peas are cooked together with a few spices to impart a subtle and distinctive flavour.

ঌ **Prep. time : 10 mins.** ঌ **Cooking time : 20 mins.** ঌ **Serves 4.**

1½ cups potatoes, boiled, peeled and diced
1 cup green peas, boiled
½ cup cumin seeds (jeera)
¾ cup onions, chopped
1 teaspoon ginger paste
1 teaspoon green chilli paste
½ teaspoon garlic paste
1 cup tomatoes, chopped
a pinch turmeric powder (haldi)
½ teaspoon chilli powder
½ teaspoon garam masala
2 tablespoons oil
salt to taste

ঌ **For the garnish**
1 tablespoon chopped coriander

1 Heat the oil and add the cumin seeds and allow them to crackle. When they crackle, add the onions and sauté till they are translucent.
2 Add the ginger paste, green chilli paste, garlic paste and tomatoes and simmer till the tomatoes are cooked.
3 Add the turmeric powder, chilli powder, garam masala, green peas and potatoes and cook for some time.
4 Add 1½ cups of water and salt and allow it to come to a boil.
5 Mash 2 to 3 pieces of potatoes in the pan to thicken the gravy. Simmer till the gravy thickens.
6 Garnish with the coriander and serve hot with rotis or parathas.

Makai Kumbh Jalfrazie

Jalfrazie is usually a dish with green chillies, capsicum and onions as the base. I have used my favourite combination of corn kernels and mushrooms as the main ingredients but if these are not your favourites, feel free to use any other vegetables of your choice.

🕊 **Prep. time : 15 mins.** 🕊 **Cooking time : 20 mins.** 🕊 **Serves 4.**

1½ cups mushrooms, quartered
¾ cup sweet corn kernels, boiled
½ cup capsicum, diced
1 teaspoon cumin seeds (jeera)
1 cup onions, chopped
1 teaspoon green chillies, chopped
2 teaspoons ginger, chopped
1 teaspoon coriander seed (dhania) powder
1 teaspoon chilli powder
1 cup tomatoes, blanched and chopped
2 tablespoons tomato ketchup
a pinch sugar (optional)
2 tablespoons oil
salt to taste

🕊 **For the garnish**
1 tablespoon chopped coriander

1. Heat the oil and add the cumin seeds. When they crackle, add the onions and sauté till they are translucent.
2. Add the green chillies, ginger, coriander seed powder and chilli powder and sauté for a few seconds.
3. Add the tomatoes and tomato ketchup and cook for another 2 to 3 minutes.
4. Add the mushrooms, corn kernels, capsicum, ¾ cup of water, sugar and salt and simmer till the mushrooms are cooked and the gravy has thickened.

Serve hot garnished with the coriander.

Soya Kofta Curry

A very interesting way to include soya in our diet. The mint flavoured koftas will surely please even those who do not enjoy eating soya.

🐚 **Prep. time : 15 mins.** 🐚 **Cooking time : 45 mins.** 🐚 **Serves 4.**

🐚 **For the soya koftas**

½ cup soya granules
½ cup boiled mashed potatoes
½ teaspoon ginger-green chilli paste
1 tablespoon chopped mint
1 tablespoon Bengal gram flour (besan)
salt to taste
oil for deep frying

🐚 **For the gravy**

1 cup onions, finely chopped
½ teaspoon ginger, grated
½ teaspoon garlic, grated
¼ cup fresh tomato purée
1 teaspoon fennel (saunf) powder
¼ teaspoon turmeric powder (haldi)
1 tablespoon coriander-cumin
seed (dhania-jeera) powder
1 teaspoon chilli powder
2 tablespoons chopped mint
¾ cup milk
½ teaspoon garam masala
1 tablespoon oil
salt to taste

🐚 **For the garnish**

10 to 12 mint leaves

Top: Bhindi Do Pyaza, page 33
Bottom: Jhatpat Subzi, page 19

For the soya koftas

1. Heat ½ cup of water in a pan, add the soya granules and allow them to soak for 5 to 7 minutes.
2. Drain out all the water by squeezing it out of the granules.
3. Combine all the ingredients in a bowl and knead into a soft dough without using any water.
4. If the dough seems soft, add more besan to adjust the consistency.
5. Divide into 10 equal portions and deep fry in hot oil till they are golden brown.
6. Drain and keep aside.

For the gravy

1. Heat the oil in a non-stick pan and add the onions.
2. Sauté the onions over a slow flame till they are golden brown.
3. Add the ginger and garlic and sauté for 1 to 2 minutes.
4. Add the tomato purée, fennel powder, turmeric powder, coriander-cumin seed powder and chilli powder and sauté till the oil separates from the gravy.
5. Add the mint and milk and bring to a boil
6. Simmer for 4 to 5 minutes. Cool completely.
7. Purée the gravy and pour it back into a pan. Add the garam masala, salt and aprrox. ½ cup of water and allow it to come to a boil.

How to proceed

Add the koftas to the gravy and simmer for 2 to 3 minutes.
Serve immediately garnished with the mint leaves.

Bhindi Do Pyaza

Picture on page 31

"Do pyaza" denotes presence of double the quantity of onions than that found in any other style of preparation. The curds added towards the end of this dish add more sharpness to this dish.

ඟ **Prep. time : 10 mins.** ඟ **Cooking time : 15 mins.** ඟ **Serves 4.**

3 cups bhindi (ladies finger), sliced
1½ cups onions, chopped
3 teaspoons cumin seeds (jeera)
1 teaspoon nigella seeds (kalonji)
¼ teaspoon turmeric powder (haldi)
3 teaspoons ginger paste
1 to 2 green chillies, chopped
¾ cup thick curds, whisked
3 tablespoons oil
salt to taste

1. Heat the oil in a pan, add the cumin seeds and nigella seeds and allow the seeds to crackle.
2. Add the onions, turmeric powder, ginger paste and green chillies and cook till the onions are tender.
3. Add the bhindi and salt and cook over a medium flame till the bhindi is tender.
4. Add the whisked curds and cook till the curds dry out.

Serve hot with parathas or rotis.

Handy tip : Bhindi tends to get sticky while cooking. Do not cover the pan while cooking and the stickiness will dry out without the presence of steam. Cook the bhindi over a slow flame for best results.

Paneer Pasanda

As the name suggests "Pasanda" means the every one is favourite. Though this recipe calls for extra effort, it is my favourite because the rich gravy wins me praise every time I make it.

❧ **Prep. time : 20 mins.** ❧ **Cooking time : 20 mins.** ❧ **Serves 4.**

1½ cups paneer, cubed

❧ For the onion and cashew paste
1 cup onions, roughly chopped
5 cloves garlic
12 mm. (½") piece ginger
2 tablespoons cashewnuts, broken

❧ For the brown onion paste
2 onions, sliced
oil for deep frying

❧ Other ingredients
1 teaspoon chilli powder
½ teaspoon garam masala
1 cup curds, whisked
salt to taste
2 tablespoons oil or ghee

❧ For the garnish
2 teaspoons cream

❧ For the onion and cashew paste
1. Boil the onions in 1 cup of water until soft.
2. Add the garlic, ginger and cashewnuts and grind into a paste.

❧ For the brown onion paste
Deep fry the onions in oil until golden brown. Drain. Grind into a fine paste in a blender using a little water.

❧ How to proceed
1. Heat the oil in a pan. Add the onion and cashew paste and cook over a slow flame for a few minutes.
2. Add the chilli powder and garam masala, mix and cook again till the oil separates from the gravy.
3. Take the pan off the fire, add the curds and mix well.
4. Simmer for 5 to 6 minutes, while stirring continuously.
5. Add the brown onion paste and salt and simmer for another 2 minutes.
6. Add the paneer, garnish with the cream and serve hot.

Hariyali Cheese Subzi

Quick, simple and nutritious- what more could you ask for an easy mid-week meal? This recipe tastes simply superb with rotis and also makes a great stuffing for parathas.

❧ Prep. time : 10 mins. ❧ Cooking time : 10 mins. ❧ Serves 2.

2 cups spring onions (including greens), chopped
2 cups spinach (palak), chopped
a pinch ajwain (carom seeds)
1 teaspoon chopped garlic
1 to 2 green chillies, finely chopped
¼ cup cheese, grated
1 tablespoon oil
salt to taste

1. Heat the oil, add the ajwain, garlic and green chilli.
2. Add the spring onions and sauté for 2 to 3 minutes.
3. Add the spinach and salt and cook for 3 to 4 more minutes over a high flame.
4. Reduce the flame and add the cheese and simmer for a few minutes.

Serve hot with chapatis.

Baingan Bharta

Chargrilled brinjals cooked with a simple combination of spices and herbs. Every region in India has their own version of baingan bharta…..this is one that's special to the North.

Select large brinjals with a shiny smooth surface as these are more likely to be without many seeds. You can also microwave these brinjals instead of cooking them over the flame at step 1.

∾ Prep. time : 5 mins. ∾ Cooking time : 30 mins. ∾ Serves 4.

1 large (750 gms) brinjals (baingan)
1 teaspoon cumin seeds (jeera)
1/2 cup onions, chopped
1 1/2 teaspoons ginger, grated
1 teaspoon garlic, grated
1 teaspoon green chillies, finely chopped
1/2 cup tomatoes, finely chopped
1/2 teaspoon turmeric powder (haldi)
1 tablespoon coriander-cumin seed (dhania-jeera) powder
1/2 teaspoon garam masala
1 tablespoon ghee
salt to taste

∾ For the garnish
2 tablespoons chopped coriander

1. Grease the brinjal with a little oil, make slits all over the surface and cook over an open flame till it is soft.
2. Cool and peel the skin. Mash the pulp thoroughly and keep aside.
3. Heat the ghee and add the cumin seeds. When they crackle add the onions and sauté for a few minutes.
4. Add the ginger, garlic and green chillies and fry again for a few seconds.
5. Add the tomato, turmeric powder, coriander-cumin seed powder and cook till the oil separates from the masala.
6. Add the mashed brinjal, garam masala and salt and mix well.

Serve hot garnished with the coriander.

GUJARATI

Gujarati cuisine has perhaps, truly perfected the art of vegetarian cooking. Even the simplest of ingredients are transformed into mouthwatering delicacies. It is a subtle blend of flavours and textures.

A traditional Gujarati thali, served on silver platters to the accompaniment of rice and a variety of wheat breads, is an "experience" in itself. Beginning with cumin spiked buttermilk, followed by hot fluffy rotlis, accompanied by a variety of lentils and pulses (kathol), vegetables, curds, pickles, farsan, mithai and finished off with rice or khichdi, it is truly a gastronomical delight.

The Gujarati food is different from most all-Indian cuisines in that the Gujaratis serve their sweets with the meal. This is also a reason why there is more sweet and sour taste in their dishes. All three regions of Gujarat have their own unique culinary styles. Kathiawar is famous for its dairy produce and pickles, while Ahmedabad is known for its dhoklas, theplas and dhebras as grains are abundantly cultivated in this region. Surat, in Southern Gujarat contributes fresh vegetable based dishes like oondhiya as this region is where vegetables grow in the arid Gujarati terrain. Gujrati subzian like Sev Tameta and the all-vegetable encompassing oondhiya are a must with their meals.

Methi Papad

A tasty vegetable dish that can be made in a jiffy. You can start making this recipe while dinner is being served and it will be ready before any other are heated. Serve it immediately as re-heating this dish is not a good idea.

→ Prep. time : 5 mins. → Cooking time : 10 mins. → Serves 2.

½ cup fenugreek (methi) leaves, chopped
2 large papads, torn into small pieces
¼ teaspoon mustard seeds (rai)
¼ teaspoon cumin seeds (jeera)
¼ teaspoon asafoetida (hing)
¼ teaspoon turmeric powder (haldi)
1 teaspoon coriander seed (dhania) powder
½ teaspoon chilli powder
1 teaspoon sugar
1 tablespoon oil
salt to taste

1. Heat the oil in a pan and add the mustard seeds and cumin seeds. When the seeds crackle, add the asafoetida.
2. Add the fenugreek leaves and sauté for 3 to 4 minutes.
3. Add the turmeric powder, coriander seed powder, chilli powder, sugar, salt and 1½ cups of water. Bring to a boil.
4. Add the papads and cook for 2 to 3 minutes.
Serve hot.

Stuffed Bhavnagri Chillies

These delectable moong dal stuffed chillies can double up as elegant starters and also make a great side vegetable when served with dal and rice.

Bhavnagri chillies are a large variety of mild green chillies. You can substitute these chillies with capsicum if you like!

❧ **Prep. time : 15 mins.** ❧ **Cooking time : 30 mins.** ❧ **Serves 4 to 6.**

8 to 10 Bhavnagri chillies, slit lengthwise and deseeded

❧ For the stuffing
½ cup moong dal (split yellow gram), soaked and boiled

½ teaspoon cumin seeds (jeera)

a pinch asafoetida (hing)

½ cup onions, chopped

2 teaspoons ginger-green chilli paste

a pinch turmeric powder (haldi)

2 tablespoons chopped coriander

2 teaspoons oil

salt to taste

❧ For the tempering
½ teaspoon cumin seeds (jeera)

1½ teaspoons oil

❧ For the stuffing

1. Heat the oil in a pan and add the cumin seeds and asafoetida.
2. When the seeds crackle, add the onions, ginger-green chilli paste and turmeric powder and sauté.
3. Add the moong dal and salt and mix well.
4. Add some water and cook till the moong dal mixture is soft and leaves the sides of the pan. Add the coriander and mix well. Keep aside.

❧ How to proceed

1. Fill the chillies with the stuffing mixture.
2. Heat the oil in a non-stick pan and add the cumin seeds.
3. When they crackle, add the chillies and sauté them over a slow flame, turning them gently till all sides are golden brown.

Serve hot with dal and rice.

Crispy Karela

Crunchy fried bitter gourds (karela) tossed with jaggery, poppy seeds and cashewnuts. This recipe tastes superb when served immediately after it is made.
It is a great accompaniment for kadhi-chawal.

≈ Prep. time : 20 mins. ≈ Cooking time : 30 mins. ≈ Serves 4.

2½ cups karela (bitter gourd), sliced
¼ cup jaggery (gur), grated
½ teaspoon cumin seeds (jeera)
¼ teaspoon asafoetida (hing)
¼ teaspoon turmeric powder (haldi)
2 tablespoons broken cashewnuts
1½ teaspoons poppy seeds (khus-khus)
½ teaspoon sesame seeds (til)
1 tablespoon raisins (kismis)
1 tablespoon oil
salt to taste

≈ Other ingredients
oil for deep frying

1. Peel and slice the karelas and apply salt over them. Cover and allow them to rest for 10 to 15 minutes. Drain out the liquid and discard.
2. Dissolve the jaggery in 3 to 4 tablespoons of water and keep aside.
3. Deep fry the karela slices in hot oil till they are crisp and golden brown. Drain and keep aside.
4. Heat 1 tablespoon of oil in a pan and add the cumin seeds. When they crackle, add the asafoetida and the turmeric powder.
5. Add the cashewnuts and fry till they are lightly browned. Then add the poppy seeds, sesame seeds and raisins.
6. Add the jaggery solution and allow it to cook for 4 to 5 minutes till it thickens. Lower the flame, mix the fried karela slices into the jaggery mixture and cook until the karlea slices are dry.
7. Transfer onto a plate and allow to cool slightly. Serve when the karela slices are crisp.

Handy tip : Save the peel of the karela to make karela theplas, just as we make mehti theplas.

Bhindi Sambhariya

Tender ladies fingers stuffed with besan and other spices make this traditional Gujarati dish a favourite. You can also stuff onions, potatoes, tendli in the same way. I often microwave this dish. This way, the bhindi stays fresh and green in colour and also cooks quickly.

❧ **Prep. time : 10 mins.** ❧ **Cooking time : 30 mins.** ❧ **Serves 4.**

250 grams bhindi (ladies fingers)
½ cup Bengal gram flour (besan)
¼ teaspoon turmeric powder (haldi)
1 teaspoon chilli powder
1 teaspoon coriander-cumin seed (dhania-jeera) powder
1 teaspoon sugar
2 tablespoons chopped coriander
½ teaspoon cumin seeds (jeera)
¼ teaspoon asafoetida (hing)
1 tablespoon oil
salt to taste

1. In a pan, combine the gram flour, turmeric powder, chilli powder, coriander-cumin seed powder and salt and cook over a medium flame till it is golden brown, stirring occasionally. Remove, cool and add the sugar and coriander.
2. Trim the ends of the bhindi and slit them lengthwise.
3. Fill these slits with the roasted gram flour mixture and cut each bhindi into 25 mm. (1") long pieces.
4. Heat the oil in a pan and add the cumin seeds. When they crackle, add the asafoetida.
5. Add the stuffed bhindi pieces and salt and cook, uncovered, over a medium flame for 10 to 15 minutes till they are done.

Serve hot.

Handy tip : Instead of the besan add ¼ cup of grated coconut and coriander each.

Turia Dhokli

A fibre filled variation of a Gujarati dish called dal dhokli, that is almost a one dish meal.
The wheat dumplings also help to thicken the gravy while the ridge gourd adds nutritional value and fibre to this dish. You can also substitute the turia with French beans or mixed vegetables.

৯০ **Prep. time : 20 mins.** ৯০ **Cooking time : 20 mins.** ৯০ **Serves 4.**

৯০ For the dhokli
½ cup whole wheat flour (gehun ka atta)
2 tablespoons besan (Bengal gram flour)
½ teaspoon chilli powder
a pinch turmeric powder (haldi)
1 tablespoon oil
1 tablespoon chopped coriander
salt to taste

৯০ Other ingredients
1½ cups turia (ridge gourd), peeled and cubed
¼ teaspoon asafoetida (hing)
¼ teaspoon turmeric powder (haldi)
½ teaspoon chilli powder
½ teapsoon ginger-green chilli paste
½ teaspoon sugar
1 teaspoon oil
salt to taste

৯০ For the dhokli
1. Combine all the ingredients in a bowl and knead into a firm dough.
2. Divide into 3 equal parts and roll out each portion into a chapati, approx. 175 mm. (7") in diameter.
3. Lightly roast each chapati on a tava till both sides are half cooked. Cool.
4. Cut each chapati into diamond shapes (approx. 1" in length) and keep aside.

৯০ How to proceed
1. Heat the oil and add the asafoetida.
2. Add the turia, turmeric powder and salt and sauté for a few seconds.
3. Add 2 cups of water, chilli powder, ginger-green chilli paste and bring to a boil.
4. Simmer till the turia is cooked.
5. Add the sugar and mix well.
6. Just before serving, bring the vegetable to a boil. Add the dhokli pieces, and add more water if required so that there enough liquid in the gravy.
7. Boil for 5 to 7 minutes till the dhokli is cooked and serve immediately.

Batata Chips Nu Shaak

Fried potatoes sautéed with khus-khus and til, slightly sweet and salty in taste. Served traditionally aamras and puri to make a delicious Sunday meal.

🙚 **Prep. time : 10 mins.** 🙚 **Cooking time : 20 to 25 mins.** 🙚 **Serves 4.**

4 large potatoes, peeled and cut into strips
oil for deep frying

🙚 **Other ingredients**
3 tablespoons cashewnuts
½ teaspoon cumin seeds (jeera)
1 teaspoon poppy seeds (khus-khus)
1 teaspoon sesame seeds (til)
½ teaspoon turmeric powder (haldi)
1 teaspoon chilli powder
1 teaspoon sugar
juice of ½ lemon
1½ tablespoons oil
salt to taste

1. Deep fry the potato strips in oil till golden brown. Drain and keep aside.
2. In another pan, heat the oil, add the cashewnuts and fry till they are golden brown
3. Lower the heat, add the cumin seeds, poppy seeds, sesame seeds, turmeric powder and chilli powder and stir well.
4. Toss in the fried potatoes, add the sugar, lemon juice and salt and mix well.
5. Stir till the sugar dissolves and then turn off the heat.
Serve hot.

Handy tip : Do not cover this dish while it is hot because the steam it releases will make the potatoes soggy.

Panchkutyu Shaak

Picture on page 49

This authentic Gujarati preparation comprises of five types of vegetables cooked in a coriander and coconut masala.

❧ **Prep. time : 10 mins.** ❧ **Cooking time : 20 mins.** ❧ **Serves 4.**

½ cup French beans, string and cut into 25 mm. (1″) pieces
½ cup turia (ridge gourd), peeled and sliced
½ cup kand (purple yam) peeled and cubed
½ cup green peas, boiled
6 to 8 baby potatoes, peeled and cubed
1 teaspoon cumin seeds (jeera)
½ teaspoon mustard seeds (rai)
¼ teaspoon asafoetida (hing)
2 teaspoons ginger-green chilli paste
a pinch turmeric powder (haldi)
2 teaspoons coriander-cumin seed (dhania-jeera) powder
½ cup coconut, grated,
½ cup chopped coriander
1 teaspoon sugar
2 tablespoons oil
salt to taste

❧ **For the methi muthia**
¼ cup fenugreek (methi) leaves
¼ cup Bengal gram flour (besan)
½ tablespoon whole wheat flour (gehun ka atta)
½ teaspoon ginger-green chilli paste
a pinch turmeric powder (haldi)
a pinch asafoetida (hing)
salt to taste
1 tablespoon oil
oil for deep frying

› For the methi muthia

1. Combine all the ingredients in a bowl and knead them together to make a soft dough (add water only and if required).
2. Divide into 8 to 10 equal parts and shape into small cylindrical rolls.
3. Deep fry in hot oil over a medium flame. Drain on absorbent paper and keep aside.

› How to proceed

1. Heat the oil and add the mustard seeds.
2. When they crackle, add the asafoetida.
3. Add all the vegetables, except the peas, salt, turmeric powder, ginger-green chilli paste, coriander-cumin seed powder and 2 cups of water and bring to a boil.
4. Simmer till the vegetables are almost cooked and the water has almost dried out.
5. Add the peas, muthia, sugar, coconut and coriander to the boiling vegetable and cook for 5 to 7 minutes till the muthias are soft.

Pressure Cooker Oondhiya

A classic Gujarati recipe, of vegetables and fenugreek dumplings cooked in an aromatic blend of spices. This version is an easy and healthy way to make oondhiya.

❧ **Prep. time : 30 mins.** ❧ **Cooking time : 60 mins.** ❧ **Serves 6.**

4 cups (½ kg.) Surti papdi, cleaned and stringed
2 cups (½ kg.) kand (purple yam)
peeled and cut into large cubes
10 to 12 (250 grams) baby potatoes, peeled
1 cup (250 grams) sweet potatoes (shakkariya),
peeled and cut into large cubes
8 to 10 (250 grams) small brinjals
3 bananas
1 recipe methi muthias (recipe below)
1 tablespoon carom seeds (ajwain)
¼ teaspoon asafoetida (hing)
2 teaspoons ginger-green chilli paste
¼ teaspoon soda-bi-carb

❧ **To be mixed together into a masala**
1 cup fresh coconut, grated
¾ cup chopped coriander
½ cup green garlic, chopped (optional)
4 teaspoons coriander-cumin seed (dhana-jeera) powder
1 tablespoon ginger-green chilli paste
2 teaspoons chilli powder
4 teaspoons sugar
1 tablespoon lemon juice
salt to taste

❧ For the methi muthias

1 cup fenugreek (methi) leaves, chopped
½ cup whole wheat flour (gehun ka atta)
½ cup Bengal gram flour (besan)
1 teaspoon ginger-green chilli paste
3 teaspoons sugar
juice of 1 lemon
½ teaspoon turmeric powder (haldi)
a pinch soda bi-carb
3 tablespoons oil
salt to taste

❧ For the tempering

¼ teaspoon asafoetida (hing)
4 tablespoons oil

❧ For the methi muthias

1. Combine all the ingredients in a bowl and knead into a soft dough, adding water only if required.
2. Divide this mixture into 30 portions and mould into oblong shapes by placing between the palms. Deep fry over a medium flame till the muthias are golden brown. Drain and keep aside.

❧ How to proceed

1. Wash the papdi, add the carom seeds, soda bi-carb and salt and mix well.
2. Make a criss-cross slit, at a right angle, in the potatoes and brinjals taking care not to separate the segments. Keep aside.
3. Cut the bananas into big pieces and cut a vertical slit in the centre of each piece.
4. Fill the masala mixture into the slits of the potatoes, brinjals and bananas. This will require about half the quantity. Keep the remaining half for later use.
5. Heat the oil for the tempering in a pressure cooker and add the asafoetida and ginger-green chilli paste.
6. Add the Surti papdi, purple yam, potatoes, sweet potatoes and brinjals and ½ cup of water and pressure cook for 2 whistles.
7. Allow the steam to escape and open the pressure cooker.
8. Transfer the cooked vegetables into a large pan and add the stuffed bananas, methi muthias and the remaining masala mixture.
9. Cook on a slow flame till the bananas are tender, stirring occasionally.

Serve hot.

Mooli Dhokli

A delectable and easy dish to make. Serve it with warm bread and salad to make a complete meal.

ॐ **Prep. time : 10 mins.** ॐ **Cooking time : 15 mins.** ॐ **Serves 4.**

2 cups radish greens, chopped
½ teaspoon cumin seeds (jeera)
1 teaspoon ginger-green chilli paste
¼ teaspoon turmeric powder
1 tablespoon dhania powder
½ teaspoon sugar
1 teaspoon oil
salt to taste

ॐ **For the dhokli**
¼ cup grated radish
¼ cup besan
2 tablespoons whole wheat flour (atta)
¼ teaspoon soda bi-carb
1½ teaspoon oil
salt to taste

ॐ For the dhokli
1. Combine all the ingredients into a dough and keep aside.
2. Divide into 20 equal portions and flatten each one between your palms and keep aside.

ॐ How to proceed
1. Heat the oil, add the cumin seeds. When they crackle, add the radish greens and salt sauté for a few second.
2. Add 3 cups of water and add the ginger-green chilli paste, turmeric powder.
3. Add the dhania powder, sugar and bring to boil.
4. Add the dhoklis to this boiling vegetables and allow them to come to the surface. Serve hot with chapatis.

Top: Puris, page 120
Bottom: Panchkutyu Shaak, page 44

Methi Besan

A traditional Gujarati recipe- a dry vegetable prepared using a combination of fenugreek leaves and Bengal gram flour tossed with spices.

Prep. time : 10 mins. Cooking time : 15 mins. Serves 4.

1½ cups fenugreek leaves (methi), chopped
½ cup Bengal gram flour (besan)
1 teaspoon ginger-green chilli paste
½ teaspoon cumin seeds (jeera)
¼ teaspoon asafoetida (hing)
¼ teaspoon turmeric powder (haldi)
1 tablespoon coriander seed (dhania) powder
½ teaspoon chilli powder
1 teaspoon sugar
2 tablespoons oil
salt to taste

1. Heat the oil and add the cumin seeds, when they crackle, add the ginger-green chilli paste and asafoetida.
2. Add the fenugreek leaves and salt and sauté for 2 to 3 minutes.
3. Add the gram flour, turmeric powder and coriander seed powder and mix well.
4. Cook over a slow flame for 10 minutes till the mixture is dry, continue to stir the mixture, occasionally.
5. Add the sugar, 2 tablespoons water and cook it for 2 to 3 more minutes till the sugar dissolves.

Serve hot.

Vatana Makai Nu Shaak

A simple and colourful vegetable dish, where the gravy is thickened using peanuts and coconut.

Prep. time : 10 mins. Cooking time : 10 mins. Serves 4.

¾ cup green peas, boiled
¾ cup sweet corn kernels, boiled
½ teaspoon cumin seeds (jeera)
½ cup capsicum, finely chopped
½ cup peanuts, crushed
1 teaspoon ginger-green chilli paste
¼ cup grated coconut
¼ teaspoon turmeric powder
½ cup tomatoes, grated
1½ teaspoons oil
salt to taste

1. Heat the oil and add the cumin seeds. When they crackle, add the capsicum and sauté for a few seconds.
2. Add the peanuts and sauté for a few seconds till they are lightly browned.
3. Add 1 cup of water, ginger-green chilli paste, coconut, turmeric powder and salt and simmer for a few minute.
4. Add the tomatoes and cook for 2 to 3 more minutes.

Serve hot with Padwali Rotis, page 111.

Sev Tameta

Tomatoes tempered with mustard seeds and ginger and served with sev. Sev is fine vermicelli made from deep-fried gram flour paste.

🐚 **Prep. time : 10 mins.** 🐚 **Cooking time : 10 to 12 mins.** 🐚 **Serves 4.**

3 cups tomatoes, chopped
½ teaspoon cumin seeds (jeera)
½ teaspoon asafoetida (hing)
½ teaspoon chopped ginger
½ teaspoon turmeric powder (haldi)
1½ teaspoons coriander-cumin seed (dhana-jeera) powder
1 teaspoon sugar
1½ cups thick sev
2 tablespoons oil
salt to taste

1. Heat the oil, add the cumin seeds, asafoetida and ginger and stir 30 seconds.
2. Add the tomatoes, turmeric powder, coriander-cumin seed powder, sugar and salt and simmer for a while.
3. Just before you wish to serve, add the sev and mix well.
Serve hot with chapatis.

Handy tip : Make this as close to serving time as possible.

RAJASTHANI

Rajasthan, the land of Rajas and Maharajas, where royalty ensured the development of a variety of beautiful arts and crafts… and of course, an array of mouth-watering food traditions. The cuisine of this state resonates with vitality and good cheer, despite the fact that its people have to struggle hard to draw up even the simplest menu from one of the harshest terrains of India.

Rajasthani food gives an insight of the rich tastes of the erstwhile royalty of this region. Cooked in pure ghee, it is famous for it's mouth- watering aroma. Lifestyle of its inhabitants and the scarcity of ingredients in the desert region has resulted in food that could last for several days and could be eaten without heating, a boon for the wanderers and nomads. Scarcity of water and lack of fresh green vegetables also had their effect on Rajasthani kitchen. They have ingeniously adapted their cooking to do without fresh vegetables too and so use amchur instead of tomatoes, dried methi instead of fresh and also made innovative dishes like Gatte Ki Subzi.

Methi Pakoda Kadhi

Picture on page 89

The perfect dish to serve for a holiday lunch. Fenugreek dumplings are deep fried and dunked for a few seconds in milk and then immersed in the curd kadhi. This process of soaking the fenugreek dumplings in milk makes them softer and more succulent and reduces the sharpness of the curd based kadhi.

Prep. time : 15 mins. Cooking time : 20 mins. Serves 4.

For the methi pakodas

½ cup fenugreek (methi) leaves
¼ cup curds, beaten
¾ cup Bengal gram flour (besan)
a pinch soda bi-carb
salt to taste

Other ingredients

¾ cup milk
oil for deep frying

For the kadhi

1 cup fresh curds, beaten
2 tablespoons Bengal gram flour (besan)
1 teaspoon cumin seeds (jeera)
a pinch asafoetida (hing)
5 curry leaves
$\frac{1}{3}$ cup onions, sliced
2 cloves garlic, finely chopped
¼ teaspoon turmeric powder (haldi)
1 tablespoon oil
salt to taste

For the methi pakodas

1. Combine all the ingredients and mix into a thick batter, using a little water.
2. Deep fry spoonfuls of the batter in hot oil, till they are golden brown in colour.
3. Drain on absorbent paper.

For the kadhi

1. Mix the curds and gram flour in a bowl, add 1 cup of water and whisk well till no lumps remain. Keep aside.
2. Heat the oil in a pan and add the cumin seeds. When they crackle, add the asafoetida, curry leaves, onions and garlic and sauté for 4 to 5 minutes.
3. Add the curds and gram flour mixture, turmeric powder and salt and bring to a boil over a slow flame.

How to proceed

1. Soak the pakodas in the milk for a few seconds. Drain and add to hot kadhi.
2. Bring to a boil and serve immediately.

Mutter Aur Chenne Ke Kofte

Paneer is also called chenna in Marwar and in this recipe they make sumptuous koftas that are simmered with green peas in a tangy gravy.

🪷 **Prep. time : 15 mins.** 🪷 **Cooking time : 20 mins.** 🪷 **Serves 4.**

½ cup green peas, boiled

🪷 For the chenna koftas
1 cup paneer (cottage cheese), grated
1½ tablespoons plain flour (maida)
a pinch of soda bi-carb
2 green chillies, finely chopped
2 tablespoons chopped coriander
salt to taste
oil for deep frying

🪷 For the garnish
1 tablespoon chopped coriander

🪷 For the gravy
½ cup curds, beaten
1 teaspoon Bengal gram flour (besan)
¼ teaspoon turmeric powder (haldi)
1½ teaspoons chilli powder
½ teaspoon cumin seeds (jeera)
2 green chillies, chopped
1 teaspoon ghee
salt to taste

🪷 For the chenna balls
1. Combine the paneer, plain flour, soda bi-carb, green chillies, coriander and salt. Knead well. Divide the mixture into 10 equal portions and shape into even sized rounds.
2. Deep fry the chenna balls in hot oil till they are golden brown.
3. Drain on absorbent paper. Keep aside.

🪷 For the gravy
1. Combine the curds, gram flour, turmeric powder and chilli powder with 1 cup of water in a bowl and mix well.
2. Heat the ghee in a pan and add the cumin seeds.
3. When they crackle, add the curds mixture, green chillies and salt and bring to a boil, stirring continuously.
4. Just before serving, add the koftas and green peas and bring to a boil.
Serve hot garnished with the coriander.

Gatte Ki Subzi

Gram flour dumplings flavoured with dry spices, steamed and then dunked into a yoghurt based curry is a traditional Rajasthani speciality. Enjoy this dish either with puris or steamed rice.

Prep. time : 20 mins. ∞ Cooking time : 25 mins. ∞ Serves 4.

∞ For the gattas
¾ cup Bengal gram flour (besan)
1 teaspoon chilli powder
1 teaspoon fennel seeds (saunf)
1/8 teaspoon ajwain (carom seeds)
1 tablespoon curds
2 tablespoons oil
salt to taste

∞ For the kadhi
2 cups curds, beaten
1 tablespoon Bengal gram flour (besan)
4 to 6 curry leaves
1 teaspoon cumin seeds (jeera)
½ teaspoon mustard seeds (rai)
½ teaspoon fennel seeds (saunf)
¼ teaspoon asafoetida (hing)
1 bay leaf (tej patta)
1 clove (laung)
25 mm. (1") stick cinnamon (dalchini)
1 cardamom (elaichi)
¼ teaspoon turmeric powder (haldi)
2 teaspoons chilli powder
2 teaspoons coriander (dhania) powder
2 tablespoons oil
salt to taste

∞ For the garnish
2 tablespoons chopped coriander

For the gattas

1. Combine all the ingredients for the gattas. Knead into a firm dough using 1 to 2 tablespoons of water.
2. Divide the mixture into 8 equal portions and shape each portion into a 75 mm. (3") long cylindrical roll.
3. Boil plenty of water in a pan and cook the gattas in boiling water for 7 to 8 minutes till they float on top. Drain and keep aside.
4. Cut the gattas into 12 mm. (½") long pieces. Keep aside.

For the kadhi

1. Combine the beaten curds, gram flour, ½ cup of water and curry leaves and mix well so that no lumps remain.
2. Heat the oil in a pan, add the cumin seeds, mustard seeds, fennel seeds, asafoetida, bay leaf, clove, cinnamon and cardamom.
3. When the seeds crackle, add the turmeric powder, chilli powder and coriander powder and sauté for a few seconds.
4. Add the curd mixture, 1 cup of water and salt and bring to a boil while stirring continuously, so that the kadhi does not split. Simmer for about 10 minutes and keep aside.

How to proceed

1. Add the prepared gattas to the kadhi and bring to a boil..
2. Serve hot, garnished with the coriander.

Pyaz Ki Subzi

Picture on facing page

An aromatic onion vegetable flavoured with dry masalas. It makes an excellent side dish.

Prep. time : 10 mins. ❧ **Cooking time : 10 mins.** ❧ **Serves 2.**

12 to 15 baby onions, peeled
1 teaspoon chilli powder
1 teaspoon coriander (dhania) powder
1 teaspoon fennel seeds (saunf)
¾ teaspoon amchur (dry mango powder)
2 teaspoons oil
salt to taste

1. Combine the chilli powder, coriander powder, fennel seeds, amchur and salt in a bowl and keep aside.
2. Make criss cross slits on the onions and stuff with the masala mixture.
3. Heat the oil in a non-stick pan, add the stuffed onions and cook over a slow flame for 7 to 8 minutes till the onions have softened and are lightly browned.

Serve hot.

Top: Bajra Aloo Roti, page 122
Bottom: Pyaz Ki Subzi, recipe above

Aloo Aur Kaddu Ki Subzi

Serve this Marwari subzi with urad dal puris.

🍃 **Prep. time : 15 mins.** 🍃 **Cooking time : 15 mins.** 🍃 **Serves 6.**

4½ cups (450 grams) red pumpkin (kaddu), cubed
4½ cups (450 grams) potatoes, chopped
2 bay leaves
12 mm. (½") stick cinnamon (dalchini)
2 cloves (laung)
2 cardamoms (elaichi)
1 teaspoon nigella seeds (kalonji)
½ teaspoon mustard seeds (rai)
½ teaspoon fenugreek (methi) seeds
2 tablespoons fresh curds, beaten
1/4 teaspoon asafoetida (hing)
1 teaspoon chilli powder
2 teaspoons coriander-cumin seed (dhania-jeera) powder
½ teaspoon turmeric powder (haldi)
½ cup tomatoes, chopped
1 teaspoon amchur powder (dry mango powder)
½ teaspoon sugar
3 tablespoons ghee
salt to taste

1. Heat the ghee and add the bay leaves, cinnamon, cloves, cardamom, nigella seeds, mustard seeds and fenugreek seeds.
2. When the seeds begin to crackle. Add the curds, asafoetida, chilli powder, coriander-cumin seed powder and turmeric powder and fry for 2 to 3 minutes.
3. Add the tomato and cook for 1 minute.
4. Add the potatoes, pumpkin and ½ cup of water, cover and cook over a medium flame for 10 to 12 minutes or until the vegetables are tender.
5. Add the amchur powder, sugar and salt and mix well.

Serve hot.

Makai Ki Subzi

Corn is one of the extensively cultivated crops in Rajasthan. The yellow sweet corn used in this recipe provides a slightly sweet taste to this vegetable which is favoured by many people.

🙿 **Prep. time : 10 mins.** 🙿 **Cooking time : 15 mins.** 🙿 **Serves 4.**

2 cups sweet corn kernels, boiled
¼ teaspoon cumin seeds (jeera)
½ teaspoon nigella seeds (kalonji)
1 teaspoon chillies, finely chopped
½ cup curds
1 teaspoon Bengal gram flour (besan)
¼ teaspoon turmeric powder (haldi)
1 teaspoon oil
salt to taste

🙿 **To be ground together into a paste**
1 cup onions, finely chopped
1 teaspoon ginger, grated
1 teaspoon garlic, grated

🙿 **For the garnish**
2 tablespoons chopped coriander

1. Combine the curds and gram flour and whisk well. Keep aside.
2. Heat the oil and add the cumin seeds and nigella seeds.
3. When the cumin seeds crackle, add the ground paste and chillies and sauté for 2 to 5 minutes over a slow flame till the mixture turns translucent.
4. Add the curds and gram flour mixture and mix well.
5. Bring to a boil while stirring continuously and add the turmeric powder and salt.
6. Add the corn and mix well and cook for a few minutes.
Serve hot, garnished with the coriander.

Kaddu Ka Bharta

This dish is proof that even with a single vegetable in hand, you can still whip up an enticing main course. Enjoy this vegetable with chapatis!

ᔛ **Prep. time : 10 mins.** ᔛ **Cooking time : 20 mins.** ᔛ **Serves 2.**

2 cups red pumpkin (kaddu), chopped
½ teaspoon cumin seeds (jeera)
½ teaspoon fennel seeds (saunf)
¼ teaspoon nigella seeds (kalonji)
a pinch fenugreek (methi) seeds
¼ cup onions, finely chopped
a pinch asafoetida (hing)
¼ teaspoon turmeric powder (haldi)
1 teaspoon chilli powder
1½ teaspoons amchur (dry mango powder)
1 tablespoon oil
salt to taste

ᔛ **For the garnish**
2 tablespoons chopped coriander

1. Heat the oil in a pressure cooker and add the cumin seeds, fennel seeds, nigella seeds and fenugreek seeds.
2. When the seeds crackle, add the onions and sauté till they turn translucent.
3. Add the pumpkin, asafoetida, turmeric powder, chilli powder and salt with ½ cup of water and pressure cook for 2 to 3 whistles so that the pumpkin becomes mushy.
4. Add the amchur and salt and mix well. Simmer till the oil separates from the pumpkin.
Serve hot, garnished with the coriander.

HYDERABADI

Hyderabad's 400-year-old culinary history, like its culture, is a princely legacy and unmatched by any other state in India. The quintessential Hyderabadi is known for his nawabi lifestyle—a gracious but rather nonchalant way of life. However, when it comes to food, the Hyderabadi won't tolerate any sluggishness and has very exacting standards. They truly believe that "khana" is best created with "fursat" and "mohabbat".......''food is best crafted with time and love."

Of all the Muslim cuisine, Hyderabadi is the only cuisine of the sub-continent that can boast of a major vegetarian element. Some of the salient features of Hyderabadi subzian are the key flavours of coconut, tamarind, peanuts and sesame seeds in them. The key spice is chilli, which is used in abundance and is the reason for the sobriquet "Dynamite Food".

Here, food is not just something to fill the stomach; it is the very essence of life, be it the mouth watering Mustard Masala Jackfruit or the 'hot'........ Mirchi ka Salan!!

Palak Makai Khaas

Sweet corn kernels tossed in an aromatic spinach gravy has a brisk flavour of toasted coconut. Serve this Hyderabadi vegetable with fresh hot parathas. Corn can also be substituted with cubes of fresh paneer, baby corn or a combination of garden fresh veggies of your choice.

Prep. time : 10 mins. Cooking time : 25 mins. Serves 4.

1½ cups sweet corn kernels, boiled
4 cups spinach, chopped
1 teaspoon cumin seeds (jeera)
¼ teaspoon asafoetida (hing)
½ cup onions, finely chopped
1½ teaspoons ginger-green chilli paste
1 teaspoon kasuri methi (dried fenugreek leaves)
3 tablespoons desiccated coconut
½ teaspoon roasted cumin seeds (jeera) powder
2 tablespoons oil
salt to taste

1. Blanch the spinach in boiling water for 2 to 3 minutes. Drain and pour cold water to refresh the spinach. Drain again.
2. Purée the spinach in a blender. Keep aside.
3. Heat the oil in a pan, add the cumin seeds and asafoetida.
4. When the seeds crackle, add the onions and ginger-green chilli paste and sauté till the onions turn translucent.
5. Add the kasuri methi and desiccated coconut and sauté till the coconut is lightly browned and crisp (approx. 4 to 5 minutes).
6. Add the puréed spinach, corn kernels, roasted cumin seed powder and salt and mix well.

Serve hot.

Mustard Masala Jackfruit

Picture on inside cover page

This recipe is from Andhra Pradesh where the food is hot and spicy. Raw jackfruit is cooked in a mustard and red chilli masala and is a must for all those who like their food spicy. Enjoy these with coorgi rotis, page 108 or rasam and rice to make a satisfying meal.

⅏ Prep. time : 15 mins. ⅏ Cooking time : 20 mins. ⅏ Serves 4.

2 cups raw jackfruit (kathal), diced
½ teaspoon turmeric powder (haldi)
salt to taste

⅏ To be ground into a paste
1 tablespoon mustard seeds (rai)
4 dry red chillies
1 teaspoon oil

⅏ Other ingredients
1 teaspoon mustard seeds (rai)
1 tablespoon split black lentils (urad dal)
1 dry red chilli, broken
8 to 10 curry leaves
1 tablespoon oil

1. Boil 2 cups of water, add the jackfruit, turmeric powder and salt and cook covered till the jackfruit is tender. Drain and discard the water.
2. Heat 1 tablespoon oil, add the mustard seeds and allow them to crackle.
3. Add the split black lentils, dry red chilli and curry leaves.
4. Add the cooked jackfruit, ground masala paste and cook for 4 to 5 minutes mixing well.

Serve hot.

Mirchi Ka Salan

A traditional Hyderabadi salan is made in a shallow wide flat bottomed handi. The salan is a sealed in this handi and kept on low fire to cook with all the flavours trapped inside to give that authentic rich taste. I have modified this recipe to suit our present day requirements, without compromising on the traditional flavours.

೪ **Prep. time : 20 mins.** ೪ **Cooking time : 20 mins.** ೪ **Serves 6.**

2 cups long green chillies (bhavnagri chillies) or capsicum, cut into thick strips

1 teaspoon cumin seeds (jeera)

½ teaspoon mustard seeds (rai)

¼ teaspoon fenugreek (methi) seeds

¼ teaspoon nigella seeds (kalonji)

6 curry leaves

¼ teaspoon turmeric powder (haldi)

2 tablespoons coriander-cumin seed (dhania-jeera) powder

2 teaspoons chilli powder

1 tablespoon tamarind (imli) pulp

2 tablespoons chopped coriander

5 tablespoons oil

salt to taste

೪ **To be ground into a dry peanut-sesame powder**

2 tablespoons peanuts, roasted

2 tablespoons sesame seeds (til), roasted

1 tablespoon cumin seeds (jeera), roasted

೪ **To be ground into a paste**

6 cloves garlic

12 mm. (½") piece ginger

½ cup onions, chopped

1 cup tomatoes, chopped

3 tablespoons fresh grated coconut

1. Wash and slit the green chillies. Remove the seeds and fry in hot oil until they turn whitish in colour. Remove and keep aside.
2. In the same oil, add the cumin seeds, mustard seeds, fenugreek seeds, nigella seeds and curry leaves.
3. When the seeds crackle, add the paste and cook for 2 minutes. Add the turmeric powder, coriander-cumin seed powder, chilli powder and powdered peanut-sesame mixture. Cook over a medium flame, stirring continuously until the oil separates.
4. Add 2 cups of water and tamarind pulp and bring it to a boil.
5. Add the fried green chillies, coriander and salt and simmer until the gravy thickens.

Serve hot.

Quick Vegetable Korma

This unusual korma is mildly spiced and has it own distinct flavour. The different vegetables used make this korma very colourful and also tasty.

› **Prep. time : 10 mins.** › **Cooking time : 20 mins.** › **Serves 4.**

¼ cup cauliflower, cut into small florets
¼ cup French beans, diced
¼ cup carrots, diced
¼ cup green peas
½ cup capsicum, diced
¼ cup baby corn, cut into slices
½ teaspoon cumin seeds (jeera)
2 medium onions, puréed
2 cloves (laung)
25 mm. (1") stick cinnamon (dalchini)
1 cardamom (elaichi)
1 teaspoon ginger-garlic paste
½ teaspoon green chilli paste
1 cup milk
¼ cup paneer (cottage cheese), cut into small pieces
¼ cup pineapple slices (canned), cut into small pieces
3 tablespoons cream
½ teaspoon garam masala
1 tablespoon ghee
salt to taste

› **For the garnish**
1 pineapple slice (canned),
cut into 4 wedges
1 tablespoon chopped coriander

1. Heat the ghee in a kadhai and add the cumin seeds. When the seeds crackle, add the onion purée, cloves, cinnamon, cardamom, ginger-garlic paste and green chilli paste and sauté for 5 to 7 minutes, while stirring continuously.
2. Add the cauliflower, French beans, carrots, green peas, capsicum, baby corn, ½ cup of milk and ¼ cup of water. Cover and cook over a slow flame till the vegetables are tender.
3. Add the remaining milk, paneer, pineapple, cream, garam masala and salt and simmer for another 3 to 4 minutes.

Serve hot garnished with the coriander and pineapple slices.

Hyderabadi Baghara Baingan

Picture on facing page

This recipe of Baghara Baingan is a traditional one and lives up to the reputation of this cuisine.

❦ **Prep. time : 15 mins.** ❦ **Cooking time : 20 mins.** ❦ **Serves 4.**

8 to 10 brinjals (small eggplants)
¼ teaspoon mustard seeds (rai)
¼ teaspoon fenugreek (methi) seeds
¼ teaspoon nigella seeds (kalonji)
8 to 10 curry leaves
3 green chillies, slit
4 tablespoons oil
salt to taste

❦ **For the garnish**
2 tablespoons chopped coriander

❦ **For the coconut and sesame paste**
2 tablespoons sesame seeds (til)
2 tablespoons fresh coconut, grated
2 tablespoons raw peanuts
1 teaspoon ginger, chopped
1 teaspoon garlic, chopped
¼ cup onions, chopped
¼ teaspoon turmeric powder (haldi)
1 teaspoon coriander seed (dhania) powder
1 teaspoon cumin seed (jeera) powder
1 teaspoon chilli powder
1 teaspoon tamarind (imli) paste

Slit the brinjals, lengthwise, into four, but leave the stems on, so the eggplants remain joined at the stem. Keep aside.

❦ For the coconut and sesame paste

1. Combine the sesame seeds, coconut, peanuts, ginger, garlic and onions in a pan and dry roast them over a slow flame till the flavours are released and the ingredients are lightly browned.
2. Add the turmeric powder, coriander seed powder, cumin seed powder, chilli powder and tamarind paste and grind it to a smooth paste using ½ cup of water. Keep aside.

❦ How to proceed

1. Heat the oil in a deep bottomed pan, add the mustard seeds, fenugreek seeds and nigella seeds.
2. When they crackle, add the brinjals, curry leaves and green chillies and sauté over medium heat for a couple of minutes. Remove and keep aside.
3. In the same pan, add the coconut and sesame paste and cook till the mixture leaves the sides of the pan.
4. Add the cooked brinjals, ½ cup of water and salt and cook covered over a slow flame till the brinjals are soft. Serve hot.

Hyderabadi Baghara Baingan, recipe above

Baby Corn Aur Paneer Ka Salan

Picture on inside cover page

The addition of crunchy baby corn and creamy soft paneer enhance the flavours and provide an interesting new twist to the recipe of a Salan. The sweet and spicy flavours marry to make a very filling and tasty main dish that requires only rotis or parathas alongside.

🌿 **Prep. time : 15 mins.** 🌿 **Cooking time : 45 mins.** 🌿 **Serves 4.**

1 cup baby corn, cut into 25 mm. (1") pieces
½ cup paneer, cut into 12 mm. (½") cubes
2 Bhavnagri chillies, sliced thickly
2 cups onions, finely chopped
2 tablespoons roasted peanuts
2 tablespoons sesame seeds (til)
2 tablespoons desiccated coconut
1 teaspoon fennel seeds (saunf)
1 teaspoon nigella seeds (kalonji)
2 teaspoons ginger-green chilli paste
1 teaspoon garlic paste
½ teaspoon chilli powder
1 teaspoon coriander seed (dhania) powder
¼ teaspoon turmeric powder (haldi)
1 cup tomatoes, finely chopped
1 teaspoon tamarind (imli), soaked in ¼ cup of water
2 teaspoons jaggery (gur), grated
4 tablespoons oil
salt to taste

🌿 **Other ingredients**
oil for deep frying

1. Boil the baby corn in water till it is cooked. Drain and keep aside.
2. Deep fry the Bhavnagri chillies in hot oil for a few seconds. Drain on absorbent paper and keep aside.
3. Heat the oil in a pan, add the onions and sauté till they turn golden brown in colour.
4. Add the peanuts, sesame seeds, desiccated coconut, fennel seeds, nigella seeds, ginger-green chilli paste, garlic paste and sauté over a slow flame till all the ingredients are browned.
5. Add the chilli powder, coriander seed powder, turmeric powder, tomatoes and salt and cook till the tomatoes soften. Cool completely.
6. Grind the gravy to a smooth paste in a blender, using a little water if required.
7. Combine the gravy with tamarind pulp and 1 cup of water and the tamarind paste and jaggerey in a pan, bring to a boil and simmer till the oil separates. Add the Bhavnagri chillies, baby corn and paneer and mix well.

Serve hot.

Handy tip : The salan has to be cooked for a long time to get the actual authentic flavour and colour of the gravy.

Yam and Spinach Pulusu

A delicious combination of yam and spinach in a tangy masala.

🔖 **Prep. time : 15 mins.** 🔖 **Cooking time : 30 mins.** 🔖 **Serves 4.**

2 cups yam (suran), peeled and cubed
2 cups spinach, chopped
1 tablespoon thick tamarind (imli) pulp
a pinch turmeric powder (haldi)
1 tablespoon roasted sesame seed (til) powder
salt to taste

🔖 To be ground into a paste
1 teaspoon mustard seeds
2 teaspoons rice
3-4 dry red chillies

🔖 For the tempering
1/4 teaspoon fenugreek (methi) seeds
1/2 teaspoon mustard seeds
1 dry red chilli, broken
6-8 curry curry leaves
2 teaspoons oil

1. Combine the yam along with the salt, turmeric powder and 1 1/2 cups of water in a pan and cook covered.
2. Once the yam is cooked add the spinach and simmer for a few minutes.
3. Add the tamarind pulp, ground paste and simmer for a few minutes.
4. Prepare the tempering by heating the oil in a pan and add the fenugreek seeds and the mustard seeds and allow them to crackle.
5. Add the dry red chilli and curry leaves and pour this tempering over the cooked yam and spinach.
6. Sprinkle the sesame seed powder and mix well.
Serve hot.

SINDHI

The Sindhi tradition is full of colour, festivity and hospitality. The Sindhi cuisine is a blend of Simple recipes, yet so delicious. That's the novelty of Sindhi Cooking! There is variety, there is taste, and there is nutrition in the simplest of foods.

The simple Sindhi Kadhi, for instance, which is a gram flour, lentil and vegetable curry, is a delicacy because the various ingredients that go into its making create a mouth-watering concoction that is also wholesome. The Sai Bhaji, another ubiquitous Sindhi dish, is as nutritious as it is famous. Spinach is the main ingredient, in addition to which there are at least eight other vegetables, pulses, and the simplest of spices. Sindhi food combines a whole lot of vegetables to produce their wholesome subzian.

Crispy Bhindi Aur Pyaz

These crisp fried ladies finger strips tossed with caramelised onions are truly delightful. Maize flour added to the bhindi makes it crisp and causes the bhindi to absorb less oil. You can use whole wheat flour (atta) or jowar flour instead of maize flour. This prepartion makes a tasty accompaniment to dal-chawal.

❧ Prep. time : 10 mins. ❧ Cooking time : 15 mins. ❧ Serves 4.

250 grams bhindi (ladies fingers)
¼ cup maize flour (makai ka atta)
2 teaspoons cumin seeds (jeera)
2 cups onions, sliced
1½ teaspoons chaat masala
2 tablespoons oil
salt to taste

❧ Other ingredients
oil for deep frying

1. Trim the ends of the bhindi and cut each bhindi into 6 to 8 strips lengthwise.
2. Apply salt on the bhindi strips and leave aside for 15 to 20 minutes.
3. Add the maize flour and toss well.
4. Deep fry the bhindi, a few pieces at a time in hot oil, till they are light brown in colour. Drain on absorbent paper and keep aside.
5. Heat the oil in a pan and add the cumin seeds. When they crackle, add the onion slices and sauté till they are lightly browned.
6. Add the fried bhindi, chaat masala and toss well.

Serve immediately.

Aloo Gobi Methi Tuk

Picture on page 107

**Crispy potaotes and cauliflower make a wonderful combination with methi leaves.
This tasty vegetable is sure to perk up any meal and it is one of my personal favourites.**

❦ **Prep. time : 15 mins.** ❦ **Cooking time : 25 mins.** ❦ **Serves 4.**

2 medium potatoes
1½ cups cauliflower, cut into florets
1 teaspoon cumin seeds (jeera)
¼ teaspoon asafoetida (hing)
1½ teaspoons ginger-green chilli paste
1 cup fenugreek (methi) leaves, finely chopped
2 teaspoons chaat masala
1 tablespoon oil
salt to taste

❦ **Other ingredients**
oil for deep frying

1. Cut the potatoes into thick wedges (lengthwise) with the skin on.
2. Deep fry the potatoes and cauliflower separately till they are golden brown. Drain on absorbent paper and keep aside.
3. Heat the oil in a non-stick pan, add the cumin seeds and asafoetida and heat.
4. When the seeds crackle, add the ginger-green chilli paste and sauté for 1 minute.
5. Add the fenugreek leaves and sauté till the leaves are crisp and lightly browned.
6. Add the fried potato and cauliflower pieces, chaat masala and salt and mix well.
Serve hot.

Handy tip : An easy way to make a simple version of chaat masala at home is to mix equal parts of black salt, roasted jeera powder and amchur powder.

Sai Bhaji

This is a recipe that a Sindhi friend of mine shared with me. There are numerous versions of this recipe and almost every Sindhi household has its own version.

⊗ Prep. time : 10 mins. ⊗ Cooking time : 25 mins. ⊗ Serves 2.

3 tablespoons split Bengal gram (chana dal)
3 cups spinach (palak), chopped
¾ cup khatta bhaji (khatta palak)
½ teaspoon cumin seeds (jeera)
⅓ cup onions, chopped
½ cup potatoes, chopped
½ cup brinjals, chopped
2 teaspoons ginger-garlic paste
1 teaspoon chilli powder
2 teaspoons coriander seed (dhania) powder
a pinch turmeric powder (haldi)
2 tablespoons oil
salt to taste

1. Combine the chana dal with 1 cup of water and pressure cook for 1 whistle. Drain the excess water and keep aside.
2. Heat the oil in a pressure cooker and add the cumin seeds.
3. When the seeds crackle, add the onions, potatoes, brinjals and ginger-garlic paste and sauté for 5 to 7 minutes.
4. Add the chilli powder, coriander seed powder, turmeric powder and salt and sauté for 2 to 3 minutes.
5. Add the spinach, khatta bhaji and the cooked chana dal and pressure cook for 2 whistles.
6. Allow to cool slightly and whisk the mixture well. Reheat and serve hot with rice or rotis.

Handy tips : Khatta bhaji is available at most vegetable vendors. It looks like a smaller version of spinach leaves and the leaves are slightly sour in taste.

Sinɔhi Kaɔhi

Sindhi cuisine is very nutritious with a predominant use of vegetables in each and every dish. Sindhi kadhi is one such example where all the vegetables are used beautifully to complement each other in taste, colour and texture.

ॐ Prep. time : 10 mins. ॐ Cooking time : 20 mins. ॐ Serves 4.

¼ cup gavarfali (cluster beans)
½ cup potato, peeled and diced
¼ cup carrots, peeled and diced
¼ cup bhindi (ladies finger), slit into 2 vertically
½ teaspoon cumin seeds (jeera)
½ teaspoon fenugreek (methi) seeds
¼ teaspoon asafoetida (hing)
4 tablespoons Bengal gram flour (besan)
2 teaspoons green chillies, chopped
1 teaspoon ginger, grated
4 to 6 curry leaves
¼ teaspoon turmeric powder (haldi)
2 teaspoons chilli powder
1 to 2 tablespoons tamarind (imli) pulp
3 tablespoons oil
salt to taste

1. Boil the gavarfali, potato and carrots in 2 cups of water till they are tender. Keep aside, retaining the water.
2. Heat the oil in another pan and add the cumin seeds and fenugreek seeds. When they crackle add the asafoetida.
3. Add the Bengal gram flour and sauté for 4 to 5 minutes over a medium flame till it is golden brown.
4. Add 4 cups of water and bring to a boil.
5. Add the green chillies, ginger, curry leaves, turmeric powder, chilli powder, tamarind pulp and all the cooked vegetables the bhindi and salt and bring to a boil. Simmer till the bhindi is cooked.

Serve hot with rice.

SOUTH INDIAN

The South Indian food is a succulent blend of flavours, colours, seasoning, nutritional balance, fragrance, taste, and visual appeal. South Indian cuisine is also hotter than its northern counterpart.

South Indian cuisine is rice based. Rice is combined with lentils to make wonderful dosas, idlis, vadas and uttapams. These items are magnificent and delicious besides being nourishing and digestible (due to the fermenting process). They are combined with *sambhar* , *rasam*, dry and curried vegetable and *pachadi* (yogurt). Their rice preparations are also masterpieces like lemon rice and rice seasoned with coconut, peanuts, tamarind, chilies, curry leaves, *urad dal* and fenugreek seeds. Here, peculiarly pulses are used as condiments. Subzian like drumsticks, baingan, suran and cabbage are part of the South Indian fare.

Coconut is also used in many forms; freshly grated, desiccated or coconut milk is added to soothe down all the fiery spices used in most of their cooking.

Mango Sasav, page 80

Mango Sasav

Picture on page 79

Sasav meaning, 'mustard seeds' in Konkani, is the main flavouring ingredients for this tantalizing sweet and sour mango dish. Traditionally, small, whole mangoes are used. You may, however, use diced mangoes (like I have done) if you prefer.

Prep. time : 10 mins.   Cooking time : 10 mins.   Serves 4.

2 cups ripe mangoes, peeled and diced
1 cup fresh coconut, grated
1 teaspoon mustard seeds (rai)
¼ teaspoon turmeric powder (haldi)
1½ teaspoons chilli powder
1½ teaspoons tamarind (imli) pulp
7 to 8 black peppercorns
2 teaspoons jaggery (gur)
salt to taste

1. Dry roast the mustard seeds in a pan till they crackle.
2. Grind together all the ingredients except the mango pieces with ½ cup water to make a paste.
3. Pour the mixture into a pan and bring to a boil.
4. Add the jaggery, salt and mango pieces and simmer for 2 minutes.
Serve hot with steamed rice.

Avial

This curry has an unusual combination of vegetables which makes the dish particularly flavourful. An ideal companion for a bowl of steaming rice.

∾ **Prep. time : 10 mins.** ∾ **Cooking time : 10 mins.** ∾ **Serves 4.**

½ cup drumsticks, cut into 25 mm. (1") pieces
½ cup french beans, diced
½ cup cauliflower florets
½ cup potatoes, cubed
½ cup green peas
½ cup brinjals, diced
2 tablespoons oil
salt to taste

∾ **For the paste**
½ cup fresh coconut, grated
1 teaspoon coriander (dhania) seeds
5 cloves garlic, crushed
3 whole dry red chillies, broken
¼ teaspoon turmeric powder (haldi)
½ teaspoon tamarind (imli) pulp
1 tablespoon oil

∾ **For the paste**
1. Heat the oil in a small pan, add the coriander seeds and garlic and sauté for 2 minutes.
2. Add the dry red chillies and sauté for 1 more minute.
3. Add this tempering to the grated coconut and grind to a smooth paste along with the turmeric powder, tamarind and a little water. Keep aside.

∾ **How to proceed**
1. Heat the oil in a pan and add the drumsticks with ¼ cup of water. Cover and cook till the drumsticks are half done.
2. Add the remaining vegetables and salt and mix well. Cover and cook till the vegetables are tender.
3. Add the paste and 1 cup of water and bring to a boil. Simmer for 5 to 6 minutes and serve hot.

Manglorean Drumstick Curry

A sweet and spicy drumstick and potato curry made the South Indian way i.e. flavoured with coconut and whole spices. This dish has a predominant garlic flavour and tastes great with steamed rice.

❧ Prep. time : 5 mins. ❧ Cooking time : 15 mins. ❧ Serves 4.

4 drumsticks, cut into 75 mm. (3") pieces
2 large potatoes, peeled and cubed
1 tablespoon jaggery (gur), grated
2 teaspoons urad dal (split black lentils)
½ teaspoon mustard seeds (rai)
10 to 12 curry leaves, torn into pieces
2 tablespoons oil
salt to taste

❧ To be ground into a smooth paste
½ cup coconut, grated
1 teaspoon cumin seeds (jeera)
4 whole red chillies, broken
2 tablespoons coriander (dhania) seeds
5 cloves garlic
2 teaspoons tamarind (imli)
½ teaspoon turmeric powder (haldi)
½ cup water

1. Cook the drumsticks and potatoes in 3 cups of water in which jaggery and salt have been added. Keep aside, retaining the water.
2. Heat the oil in a pan, add the urad dal and mustard seeds and sauté. When the seeds crackle, add the curry leaves and stir once.
3. Add the cooked drumsticks and potatoes along with 1 cup of the water in which they were cooked, the ground paste and salt (if required) and bring to a boil.
4. Simmer for 5 to 7 minutes.
Serve hot.

Potato Saung

This is a homestyle Mangalorean potato dish. Simple, yet delicious and easy to rustle up. Serve with steamed rice and curds for a quick and wholesome meal.

❧ Prep. time : 5 mins. ❧ Cooking time : 15 mins. ❧ Serves 4.

2 large potatoes
¾ cup onions, finely chopped
2 tablespoons chilli powder
1½ teaspoons thick tamarind (imli) pulp
2 tablespoons oil
salt to taste

1. Peel and cut the potatoes into thick semicircular slices.
2. Heat the oil, add the onions and sauté till they are translucent.
3. Add the chilli powder and sauté for 1 more minute.
4. Add the potatoes, salt and 1 cup of water. Cover and cook over a medium flame till the potatoes are done.
5. Add the tamarind pulp and simmer for a few more minutes.
Serve hot.

French Beans Foogath

Variation of the famous South Indian ' Beans foogath', I've added chana dal to the dish which adds to its existing flavours.

2 cups french beans, stringed and chopped
¼ cup Bengal gram (chana dal), soaked
½ teaspoon mustard seeds (rai)
1 teaspoon urad dal (spli black lentils)
4 to 6 curry leaves
¼ teaspoon asafoetida (hing)
1 teaspoon grated ginger
¼ teaspoon turmeric powder (haldi)
¼ cup fresh coconut, grated
1½ teaspoons oil
salt to taste

ೞ For the garnish
2 tablespoons chopped coriander

1. Heat the oil and add the mustard seeds. When they crackle, add the urad dal and sauté for a few seconds.
2. Add the curry leaves, asafoetida and ginger.
3. Add the French beans, chana dal, turmeric powder, salt and ¼ cup of water, mix well and cover. Cook over a medium flame for 10 to 12 minutes.
4. When the French beans and Bengal gram are tender, add the coconut and cook for 2 to 3 more minutes.

Serve hot, garnished with the coriander.

Handy tip : Select tender French beans for best results.

Plantain Errisery

Plantains (bananas) are one of the most commonly grown vegetables along the coast. This dish is very easy to make and is a wonderful accompaniment to steamed rice and dal.

Prep. time : 10 mins. Cooking time : 15 mins. Serves 4.

3 raw bananas (plantains)
¼ teaspoon turmeric powder (haldi)
2 teaspoons mustard seeds (rai)
2 teaspoons urad dal (split black lentils)
4 dry red chillies, broken
12 to 14 curry leaves
2 tablespoons fresh coconut, grated
salt to taste
2 teaspoons oil

1. Peel the bananas and cut into cubes.
2. In a pan, add the bananas, ¼ cup water, turmeric powder and salt and allow it to cook till bananas are tender and the water dries up. Keep aside
3. Heat the oil in a pan, add the mustard seeds and urad dal and allow the seeds to crackle.
4. Add the dry red chilies and curry leaves and stir for a few seconds.
5. Add the cooked bananas and grated coconut and mix well. Cook over a slow flame for 5 to 7 minutes.

Serve hot.

Cabbage Poriyal

Poriyal is any dry vegetable preparation flavoured with generous amounts of fresh grated coconut. Cabbage tempered with mustard seeds and dry red chillies makes a delightful accompaniment to any South Indian main course.

ॐ **Prep. time : 10 mins.** ॐ **Cooking time : 10 mins.** ॐ **Serves 4.**

2 cups cabbage, shredded
1 teaspoon mustard seeds (rai)
½ teaspoon urad dal (split black lentils)
1 green chilli, slit
2 dry red chillies, broken
8 to 10 curry leaves
a pinch turmeric powder (haldi)
¼ cup fresh coconut, grated
2 teaspoons oil
salt to taste

1. Heat the oil, add the mustard seeds and urad dal and allow the seeds to crackle.
2. Add the green chilli, dry red chillies, curry leaves and turmeric powder and stir for few seconds.
3. Add the cabbage, salt, ¼ cup of water and cook over a medium flame till the cabbage is tender.
4. Add the grated coconut, mix well and serve hot.

Chana Ghassi

Roasted coconut and spices are ground together to make this fragrant and traditional curry. I have used black horse gram but you may use any combination of vegetable and / or lentils of your choice.

ॐ **Prep. time : 20 mins.** ॐ **Cooking time : 15 mins.** ॐ **Serves 4.**

1 cup kala chana (black horse gram), boiled
½ cup fresh coconut, grated
25 mm. (1") cinnamon stick (dalchini)
4 cloves (laung)
3 peppercorns
3 dry red chillies
½ cup onions, sliced
salt to taste

1. Mix all the ingredients together, except the kala chana and dry roast until golden brown in colour. Allow it to cool.
2. Grind the mixture to a smooth paste with ½ cup of water.
3. Transfer the mixture to a pan and allow it come to a boil.
4. Add the boiled horse gram and salt and allow it to simmer for a few minutes.
Serve hot with steamed rice.

Handy tip : ½ **cup raw chana, when soaked and boiled will yield approx. 1 cup of boiled chana.**

Madras Onion Stew

A simple, well-seasoned stew of baby onions simmered in a spicy coconut gravy. The rich flavours of this dish are satisfying as well as healthy. Shallots or Madras onions used here are a variety of small onions that can be substituted by small white onions, if you prefer.

๛ Prep. time : 15 mins. ๛ Cooking time : 20 mins. ๛ Serves 4.

1 cup Madras onions, peeled
½ cup onions, chopped
½ teaspoon mustard seeds (rai)
a few curry leaves
¼ teaspoon asafoetida (hing)
1 cup coconut milk
1 teaspoon jaggery (gur), grated
1 teaspoon tamarind (imli) pulp
1 tablespoon oil
salt to taste

๛ To be ground into a smooth paste

2 tablespoons grated coconut
1 teaspoon chilli powder
1 tablespoon coriander (dhania) powder
4 to 6 cloves garlic
25 mm. (1") piece ginger
2 tablespoons water

1. Heat the oil and add the mustard seeds. When they crackle, add the curry leaves and asafoetida.
2. Add the Madras onions and chopped onions and sauté over a slow flame till they are lightly browned.
3. Add the ground paste and sauté till it is lightly browned.
4. Add the coconut milk, jaggery, tamarind pulp, salt and ½ cup of water and bring to a boil.
5. Simmer for 4 to 5 minutes and serve hot with appams or rice.

Handy tip : If you can not find Madras onions, use large dices of regular onion instead.

Methi Pakoda Kadhi, page 54

Ridge Gourd Upkari

A sumptuous turai vegetable prepared the Manglorean way that can be made in a jiffy.

๛ Prep. time : 5 mins. ๛ Cooking time : 10 mins. ๛ Serves 4.

2 cups turai (ridge gourd), peeled and cubed
1 teaspoon mustard seeds (rai)
2 whole dry red chillies, broken
2 green chilies, slit
6 to 8 curry leaves
¼ teaspoon asafoetida (hing)
½ cup onions, chopped
¼ cup coconut, grated
¼ teaspoon turmeric powder (haldi)
1 tablespoon oil
salt to taste

1. Heat the oil in a pan and add the mustard seeds.
2. When the mustard seeds crackle, add the dry red chillies, green chillies, curry leaves and asafoetida.
3. Add the onions and sauté till they turn translucent.
4. Add the turai, salt and ¼ cup of water, cover and cook till the turai is tender.
5. Add the coconut and turmeric powder and sauté for 2 more minutes.

Serve hot with chapatis.

Kai Kutan

A traditional preparation from Kerala where "Kai" means plantain and 'Kutan' means curry.
Coconut, cumin seeds and ginger combine with curds to make this delicious plantain curry. Enjoy this traditional recipe with steamed rice.

❀ Prep. time : 10 mins. ❀ Cooking time : 10 mins. ❀ Serves 4.

3 raw bananas
½ cup fresh coconut, grated
1 teaspoon cumin seeds (jeera)
1 green chilli
1 teaspoon ginger, chopped
a pinch turmeric powder (haldi)
¼ cup thick curds

❀ For tempering
2 teaspoons oil
2 dry red chillies
1 teaspoon mustard seeds (rai)
salt to taste

1. Grind together fresh coconut, ginger and green chilli with ¼ cup water to a paste. Keep aside.
2. Peel the bananas and cut into cubes.
3. Add ½ cup water, turmeric and salt to the banana pieces and cook till they are tender.
4. Add the coconut mixture to the cooked banana and cook for a few minutes.
5. In another pan, heat 2 teaspoons oil and add mustard seeds and let the seeds crackle.
6. Add the dry red chilli, curry leaves and cook for a few seconds.
7. Add this tempering to the banana, coconut mixture and cook for few minutes.
8. Let the banana curry cool a little, add the whisked curds and salt and mix well.
Serve immediately.

Matki Aur Palak Ki Curry

Wonderfully seasoned but not too spicy, this South Indian style vegetable is an excellent accompaniment for rice or parathas.

❧ Prep. time : 10 mins. ❧ Cooking time : 20 mins. ❧ Serves 6.

1 cup sprouted matki (moath beans)
3 cups chopped spinach (palak)
1 tomato, finely chopped
½ teaspoon mustard seeds (rai)
4 cloves garlic, crushed
10 to 12 curry leaves, torn into pieces
1 tablespoon oil
salt to taste

❧ To be ground into a smooth paste
½ teaspoon coriander (dhania) seeds
¼ teaspoon cumin seeds (jeera)
¼ teaspoon fenugreek (methi) seeds
1 clove garlic
3 whole dry red chillies, broken
¼ teaspoon turmeric powder (haldi)
¼ cup grated coconut
¼ cup water

1. Combine the sprouted matki, spinach, tomato and salt with 1½ cups of water in a pan and cook till the matki is tender.
2. Add the ground paste and simmer for 10 more minutes. Keep aside.
3. Make a tempering by heating the oil in a small pan and adding mustard seeds to it.
4. When the seeds crackle, add the garlic and sauté for 2 minutes.
5. Add the curry leaves and pour this tempering over the kari, bring it to a boil and serve hot.

MAHARASHTRIAN

Maharashtrian cuisine resonates in its simple flavours and each region in Maharashtra has their own kind of cuisine depending on its geographic location. Coastal Maharashtrian cuisine is largely dependent on freshly ground spices and use coconut abundantly. The ghat areas however use dried spices and masalas and garlic dominates. Be it the aromatic masala bhaat or the ever popular vada pav and Sabudana khichdi washed down with Piyush it's a simple yet superb cuisine.

Maharashtrian Cuisine combines the tang and spice from its coastal belt, as well as an alluringly earthy and rustic flavour from the craggy Deccan interiors. A reflection of the land of lavanis, karanjis, kothimbir vadis, Marathi food uses lots of simple ingredients, coconuts, grated coconuts, peanuts and cashew nuts are widely used in vegetables.

Their vegetable preparations are simple, flavourful and nutritious. Peanut oil is the main cooking medium. Maharashtrians mix a lot of sprouted lentils in the vegetables, along with coconut, groundnut and kokum.

Zunka

Zunka is ideal for these who love their food spicy. A Maharastrian speciality, this dish is generally served with Bhakhri and onions but you may also enjoy it with rotis if you do not care for Bhakhri.

ॐ **Prep. time : 10 mins.** ॐ **Cooking time : 20 mins.** ॐ **Serves 4.**

1¼ cups Bengal gram flour (besan)
2 cups onions, chopped
1 teaspoon mustard seeds (rai)
1 teaspoon cumin seeds (jeera)
¼ teaspoon asafoetida (hing)
2 teaspoons ginger, chopped
2 teaspoons garlic, chopped
1 teaspoon green chilli, chopped
2 teaspoons chilli powder
½ teaspoon turmeric powder (haldi)
½ cup chopped coriander
2 tablespoons oil
salt to taste

1. Heat the oil in a pan, add the mustard seeds and allow them to crackle.
2. Add the cumin seeds, asafoetida and onions and cook till the onions are tender.
3. Add the ginger, garlic and green chilli and cook for some more time.
4. Add the chilli powder, turmeric powder, Bengal gram flour and salt and cook over a slow flame till the flour is lightly browned.
5. Add 2½ cups of water, stirring continuously, till the Bengal gram flour thickens and leaves the sides of the pan. Cook over a slow flame for 4 to 5 minutes till the besan smells cooked.
6. Add the coriander and mix well.

Serve hot.

Bharleli Vaangi

Small brinjals stuffed with a sweet and spicy, peanut flavoured mixture drawing out all the authentic flavours of Maharashtrian cooking. The brinjals have to be cooked over a slow flame with utmost care in order to preserve the natural flavours of this dish.

Prep. time : 15 mins. Cooking time : 25 mins. Serves 6.

12 small brinjals (small)

For the stuffing

1¼ cups onions, sliced
2 teaspoons coriander seeds (dhania)
1 teaspoon cumin seeds (jeera)
6 peppercorns
6 cloves (laung)
25 mm. (1") stick cinnamon (dalchini)

Other ingredients

1½ cups onions, finely chopped
4 teaspoons red chilli powder
2 tablespoons tamarind (imli) pulp
½ teaspoon turmeric powder (haldi)
¼ cup unsalted peanuts, roasted and crushed
3 teaspoons jaggery (gur), grated
1 tablespoon oil
salt to taste

For the brinjals

1. Wash and dry the brinjals.
2. Slit each brinjal, once through and then again at a right angle to make 4 equal parts without separating them from the stem. Retain a small part of the stem.
3. Soak the brinjals in a bowl of salted water for 10 to 15 minutes. Then pat them dry and keep aside.

For the stuffing

Dry roast all the ingredients over a slow flame and grind to a paste with ¼ cup of water.

How to proceed

1. Mix together the onions, red chilli powder, tamarind pulp, turmeric powder, crushed peanuts, jaggery, salt and the ground paste.
2. Stuff this mixture in the brinjals and keep aside.
3. Heat the oil in a pan and place the stuffed brinjals one by one. Add ¼ cup of water, cover and cook over a slow flame till the brinjals are tender.

Serve hot.

Vaal Drumsticks

Picture on page 117

The unusual combination of field beans and drumsticks blend perfectly well to make a nutritious and tasty vegetable. You may also use a combination of doodhi and val.

🍥 **Prep. time : 5 mins.** 🍥 **Cooking time : 20 mins.** 🍥 **Serves 4.**

1 cup sprouted vaal (field beans)
2 drumsticks, cut into 25 mm. (1") pieces
½ teaspoon mustard seeds (rai)
½ teaspoon turmeric powder (haldi)
1 tablespoon oil
salt to taste

🍥 **To be ground into a paste**
2 tablespoons grated coconut
2 to 3 large cloves garlic
1 teaspoon jaggery (gur), grated

1. Heat the oil in a pan and add the mustard seeds.
2. When the mustard seeds crackle, add the vaal, salt and about ½ cup of water. Cover with a lid and cook on a medium flame till the vaal is half done.
3. Add the drumsticks, cover and cook again till the vaal and drumsticks are cooked, adding more water, if required.
4. Add the ground paste and turmeric powder and stir for 2 to 3 minutes.
5. Finally add the jaggery and simmer for a few minutes.
Serve hot.

Vegetable Kalvan

"Kalvan" is the Marathi word for a gravy-like dish. This spicy coconut based dish is a tongue tickling blend of flavours and is really easy to make.

🙠 Prep. time : 20 mins. 🙠 Cooking time : 25 mins. 🙠 Serves 4.

1 cup mixed boiled vegetables
(carrots, French beans, green peas)
½ teaspoon cumin seeds (jeera)
¼ teaspoon asafoetida (hing)
¼ cup milk
a pinch sugar
salt to taste
1 teaspoon oil

🙠 For the garnish
2 tablespoons chopped coriander

🙠 For the gravy
1 cup onions, sliced
1 tablespoon ginger, chopped
1 tablespoon garlic, chopped
4 to 6 curry leaves
¼ cup desiccated coconut
1 cup tomatoes, chopped
¼ teaspoon turmeric powder (haldi)
2 teaspoons chilli powder
1 tablespoon oil
salt to taste

🙠 For the gravy
1. Heat the oil in a pan, add the onions, ginger, garlic and curry leaves and sauté for 4 to 5 minutes over a low flame.
2. Add the desiccated coconut and allow it to brown lightly.
3. Add the tomatoes, turmeric powder, chilli powder and salt and cook till the tomatoes are cooked.
4. Cool completely and grind into a fine paste.

🙠 How to proceed
1. Heat the oil and add the cumin seeds. When they crackle, add the asafoetida and then the gravy.
2. Cook over a slow flame till the gravy thickens and the oil starts to separate from the masala.
3. Add the milk and 1 cup of water and allow it to come to a boil.
4. Add the vegetables, sugar and salt and mix well.

Serve hot, garnished with the coriander.

Shengdane Ani Vatane Chi Bhaji

Shengdane i.e. peanuts are used in many Maharashtrian dishes. Here we use peanuts and green peas as the main ingredients to make this dish with an authentic flavour.

🐚 **Prep. time : 15 mins.** 🐚 **Cooking time : 15 mins.** 🐚 **Serves 4.**

1½ cups unsalted peanuts, crushed
1 cup green peas, boiled

🐚 **To be ground to a paste**
3 tablespoons fresh coconut, grated
3 cloves (laung)
25 mm. (1") stick cinnamon (dalchini)
4 green chillies
½ cup water

🐚 **Other ingredients**
2 teaspoons cumin seeds (jeera)
2 dry red chilies, broken
a pinch sugar
2 tablespoons ghee or oil
salt to taste

🐚 **For garnish**
1 tablespoon chopped coriander

1. Heat the ghee, add the cumin seeds and cook till the seeds crackle.
2. Add the dry red chillies and crushed peanuts and cook for some time.
3. Add the coconut paste, 1 cup of water, sugar and salt and cook on low flame till the peanuts are cooked.
4. Add the green peas and simmer for 2 minutes.
Serve hot, garnished with the coriander.

Batata Chi Bhaji

A simple dish of potatoes tempered with green chillies and curry leaves and spiced up with crushed peanuts. This is also enjoyed during fasting days and is also called "Puneri Aloo".

ॐ **Prep. time : 10 mins.** ॐ **Cooking time : 10 mins.** ॐ **Serves 4.**

3 cups potatoes, boiled and diced
2 teaspoons cumin seeds (jeera)
6 to 8 curry leaves
3 green chillies, slit
3 teaspoons roasted peanuts, crushed
a pinch of sugar
2 teaspoons oil
salt to taste

ॐ **For the garnish**
1 tablespoon chopped coriander

1. Heat the oil in a pan, add the cumin seeds and allow them to crackle.
2. Add the curry leaves, green chillies and potatoes and mix well.
3. Add the peanuts, sugar and salt and mix well.
Serve hot, garnished with the coriander.

Handy tip : You can also double up the crushed peanuts and add a dash of lime juice to add more "pep" to this traditional recipe.

Batata Ani Flower Cha Rassa

A homestyle potato and cauliflower vegetable with a water gravy. It uses a blend of spices called "goda masala" is a blend of spices used in Maharashtrian cooking. It is easily available at most grocery stores.

❧ Prep. time : 10 mins. ❧ Cooking time : 15 to 20 mins. ❧ Serves 4.

1 cup potatoes, peeled and diced
1 cup cauliflower florets
½ teaspoon mustard seeds (rai)
1 teaspoon cumin seeds (jeera)
½ cup onions, chopped
¼ teaspoon turmeric powder (haldi)
½ cup tomato, chopped
1 teaspoon ginger paste
1 teaspoon garlic, chopped
1 green chilli, chopped
1 teaspoon chilli powder
¼ teapsoon goda masala or garam masala
a pinch of sugar
salt to taste
2 teaspoons oil

❧ **For the garnish**
1 tablespoon chopped coriander

1. Heat the oil, add the mustard seeds and cumin seeds and allow them to crackle.
2. Add the onions and turmeric powder and cook till the onion is translucent.
3. Add the tomato, ginger, garlic and green chilli and cook till the tomato pieces are soft.
4. Add the potatoes and 3 cups of water and simmer till the potatoes are partially done.
5. Add the cauliflower, chilli powder, goda masala, sugar and salt and cook till cauliflower and potatoes are done.
Serve hot garnished with the coriander.

Dalimbi

A traditional preparation which is a hot favourite among the Maharashtrians. The field beans are cooked with kokum which imparts a subtle hint of sour flavours that are distinctly different from using tamarind or lemon.
Kokum is the dried peel of the fruit which is grown along coast. It is easily available at most grocers.

∾ Prep. time : 10 mins. ∾ Cooking time : 25 mins. ∾ Serves 4.

2 cups sprouted vaal (field beans)
4 to 5 kokums
1 teaspoon cumin seeds (jeera)
½ teaspoon asafoetida (hing)
5 to 6 teaspoons curry leaves
1 teaspoon ginger, grated
1 cup onions, finely chopped
½ teaspoon turmeric powder (haldi)
3 teaspoons jaggery (gur), chopped
2 teaspoons chilli powder
4 tablespoons chopped coriander
1 teaspoon oil
salt to taste

1. Soak the kokums in ¼ cup of water and leave aside for 10 to 15 minutes. Purée the soaked kokums in a blender to get a smooth paste. Strain and keep aside.
2. Heat the oil in a non-stick pan and add the cumin seeds. When they crackle, add the asafoetida, curry leaves and ginger and sauté for a few seconds.
3. Add the onions and sauté till they turn translucent.
4. Add the vaal and 1 cup of water. Cover and cook for 15 minutes.
5. Add the turmeric powder, kokum paste, jaggery, chilli powder, coriander and salt and cook for another 5 minutes.

Serve hot.

Makai Patal Bhaji

This dish made with hearty chunks of corn on the cob in a sweet and spicy sauce of colocassia leaves (arvi) and Bengal gram dal.

Prep. time : 20 mins. ❧ Cooking time : 30 mins. ❧ Serves 4.

2 small corncobs, cut into 25 mm. (1") pieces, boiled
4 cups colocassia leaves, chopped
½ cup split Bengal gram (chana) dal, boiled
½ teaspoon cumin seeds (jeera)
½ teaspoon asafoetida (hing)
½ teaspoon ginger, grated
1 green chilli, chopped
¼ teaspoon turmeric powder (haldi)
1 teaspoon coriander-cumin seed (dhania-jeera) powder
2 teaspoons thick tamarind (imli) pulp
1 tablespoon jaggery (gur), grated

1. Heat the oil, add the cumin seeds, hing, ginger and green chilli.
2. Add the colocassia leaves, chana dal, turmeric, dhania-jeera and 1 cup of water and pressure cook for 3 whistles.
3. Whisk well till it is smooth.
4. Add the corncobs, tamarind pulp and jaggery and bring to a boil.
Serve hot.

Handy tip : You can also used boiled baby corn instead of the corn cobs.

Panchamrut

Panchamrut indicates the presence of 5 main ingredients in a preparation. This preparation can be enjoyed as a accompaniment and also as a main course. Serve this with varan bhat to make complete Maharashtrian meal.

Prep. time : 15 mins. Cooking time : 15 mins. Serves 4.

2 cups capsicum, diced
1 teaspoon mustard seeds (rai)
a pinch asafoetida (hing)
½ cup fresh coconut, grated
¼ cup raw peanuts, coarsely powdered
4 teaspoons sesame seeds (til), coarsely powdered
1 to 2 teaspoons chilli powder
2 tablespoons jaggery (gur), grated
2 teaspoons thick tamarind (imli) pulp
2 teaspoon oil
salt to taste

1. Heat the oil, add the mustard seeds and allow the seeds to crackle.
2. Add the asafoetida, coconut, peanuts and sesame powder and cook for some time.
3. Add the capsicum, chilli powder and cook for some time.
4. Add 1 cup water, salt, jaggery and tamarind and cook for 10 minutes till the gravy thickens.

Serve hot with chappatis.

Vegetable Kolhapuri

Picture on coverpage

This popular spicy mixed vegetable preparation has many variations. I have chosen this recipe which is the closest to the traditional one and uses a mixture of desiccated coconut along with other spices as the base for the gravy.

Prep. time : 15 mins. Cooking time : 20 mins. Makes 6.

2 cups mixed boiled vegetables
(carrots, cauliflower, French beans, green peas)
1 cup onions, finely chopped
½ cup tomatoes, finely chopped
1½ teaspoons garam masala
2 tablespoons oil
salt to taste

To be ground into a paste
¼ cup desiccated coconut
3 dry red chillies
5 cloves garlic
25 mm. (1") piece ginger
1 tablespoon khus-khus (poppy seeds)
1 tablespoon sesame seeds (til)

For the garnish
2 tablespoons chopped coriander

1. Heat the oil, add the onions and cook till the onions turn golden brown in colour.
2. Add the ground paste and tomatoes and cook till the oil separates.
3. Add the vegetables, salt, garam masala and ¾ cup water and bring it to a boil.
Serve hot garnished with the coriander.

ROTIS

Wheat, the staple diet of millions of Indians and others all over the world, is consumed in different cultures and geographical areas in different forms. In India, wheat is consumed largely in the form of preparations made from atta or maida.

No Indian bread is as versatile as the *paratha*. Parathas are originally a part of the cuisine of Avadh. They form an integral part of the elaborate traditional Lucknowi breakfast. Filled with delectable mixtures of seasonal vegetables, paneer or simply kneaded dough that is rolled and layered with ghee to make crisp and flaky lachha parathas, are guaranteed to make your mouth water. *Parathon-wali-galli* at Chandani Chowk in Delhi stands as a classic example that they are very popular among the rich and the poor alike.

Indian cuisine also boasts of a large variety of breads. This section showcases some simple recipes that will complement all the vegetable dishes in this book.

Sindhi Koki

Picture on facing page

A Sindhi specialty made with whole wheat flour kneaded with onions and coriander to make a filling roti.

🌿 **Prep. time : 10 mins.** 🌿 **Cooking time : 20 mins.** 🌿 **Makes 8 kokis.**

2 cups wheat flour (gehun ka atta)
½ cup onions, chopped
2 tablespoons chopped coriander
2 to 3 green chillies, chopped
1 teaspoon cumin seeds (jeera)
2 tablespoons melted ghee
¾ teaspoon salt

🌿 **Other ingredients**
ghee for cooking

1. Sift the flour and salt into a bowl. Add the remaining ingredients, mixing enough water to make a stiff dough.
2. Knead the dough lightly, then divide into 8 equal portions. Roll out each portion into square parathas 100 mm. x 100 mm. (4" x 4").
3. Cook each one on a hot tava and spoon ghee round the edges. While cooking, prick holes in the koki and cook until both sides are golden brown in colour.

Serve hot.

Top: Sindhi Koki, recipe above
Bottom: *Aloo Gobi Methi Tuk, page 75*

Coorgi Roti

Picture on inside coverpage

These are my favourite rotis. Soft, yet flaky these rice flour chapatis are perfect to serve with most South Indian dishes.

🍃 **Prep. time : 10 mins.** 🍃 **Cooking time : 15 mins.** 🍃 **Makes 6 rotis.**

1½ cups cooked rice
2 cups rice flour
salt to taste

🍃 **Other ingredients**
ghee for serving

1. Purée the cooked rice with a little water in a blender.
2. Add this to the rice flour and salt and knead into a dough, adding more water only if required.
3. Cover with a damp muslin cloth and keep aside for 10 to 15 minutes.
4. Divide into 6 equal portions and roll out each portion into 150 mm. (6″) diameter circle.
5. Cook each circle on a tava over medium flame till brown specks appear on the surface.

Serve hot smeared with a little ghee.

VARIATION : MASALA COORGI POORIS

1. Add the step 2, add ¼ teaspoon of chopped coriander and 1 to 2 chopped green chillies and knead it into the dough.
2. Divide the dough into 12 parts, roll out 12 puris and deep fry in hot oil.
3. Drain on absorbent paper and serve hot.

Masala Bhatura

Bhaturas are leavened puris served with Chole. They are soft and spongy and must be enjoyed while they are hot or else they become chewy.

This recipe is a different variation that uses potatoes to add softness to the bhaturas and a blend of other ingredients to flavour them. Another innovation is that I have cooked them lightly on a tava and kept them aside. Deep fry them only when you need to serve them to enjoy these hot and fresh.

❧ **Prep. time : 10 mins.** ❧ **Cooking time : 20 mins.** ❧ **Makes 6 bhaturas.**

½ cup whole wheat flour (gehun ka atta)
½ cup plain flour (maida)
½ cup boiled and mashed potato
1 tablespoon chopped coriander
2 tablespoons onions, finely chopped
1 to 2 green chillies, finely chopped
¼ teaspoon garam masala
salt to taste

❧ **Other ingredients**
oil for deep frying

1. Combine all the ingredients in a bowl and knead into a firm dough using water as required.
2. Cover with a damp muslin cloth and keep aside for 10 to 15 minutes.
3. Divide into 6 equal portions and roll each portion into a 100 mm. (4") diameter circle.
4. Cook each portion over a tava for a few seconds on each side. Keep aside.
5. Just before you wish to serve them, deep fry them in hot oil over a medium flame till they are golden brown. Drain on absorbent paper.

Serve hot.

Makhani Roti

Picture on page 11

A simple yet delicious way to make rotis. Flavoured with butter and freshly crushed black pepper this whole wheat roti is perfect to serve with most of your favourite vegetable dishes.

Prep. time : 10 mins. Cooking time : 20 mins. Makes 4.

1 cup whole wheat flour (atta)
1 tablespoon butter
½ teaspoon freshly crushed black pepper
a pinch salt

For serving
butter

1. Rub the butter into the flour using your fingertips till the consistency resembles that of breadcrumbs.
2. Add the pepper and salt and knead into a firm dough using enough water.
3. Cover with a damp muslin cloth for 10 to 15 minutes.
4. Divide the dough into 4 equal portions and roll each portion into a 100 mm. (4") diameter circle.
5. Place the roti on a hot tava and turn over in a few seconds and cook this side till the edges begin to curl slightly and small blisters appear on the surface.
6. Cook the other side for a few more seconds.

Serve hot topped with some butter.

Handy tip : Dab one side of the roti with a few drop of water so that it sticks firmly to the tava and does not fall off while turning the tava over.

Padvali Rotli

"Pad" in Gujarati means layers. This is a layered chapati, usually served with "aamras" during the mango season. Press the chapatis lightly with a soft piece of muslin cloth to make the outer 2 layers crisp.

✲ Prep. time : 10 mins. ✲ Cooking time : 20 mins. ✲ Makes 3 rotlis.

1 cup whole wheat flour (gehun ka atta)
½ teaspoon salt
1 teaspoon oil

✲ Other ingredients
1 tablespoon ghee
1 teaspoon whole wheat flour (gehun ka atta)
ghee for serving

1. Combine the flour and salt and knead into a soft and pliable dough.
2. Add the oil and knead again till the dough is smooth and elastic.
3. Cover and keep aside for 10 to 15 minutes.
4. Divide the dough into 9 equal parts.
5. Roll out each portion into a 25 mm. (1") diameter circle.
6. Layer 3 circles with a thin layer of ghee and a sprinkling of flour.
7. Repeat to make 3 chapatis of this kind.
8. Roll out each of them into a circle approx. 125 mm. (5") diameter.
9. Cook each one on a tava over a slow flame pressing it lightly with a ball of soft cloth, till both sides are lightly browned and the layers are separated.

Serve immediately smeared with a little ghee after lightly separating the layers.

Lachcha Paneer Paratha

A different way of making and cooking paneer parathas. I have cooked these on a non-stick tava by reversing the tava over the open flame just like tandoori parathas are made.

≫ **Prep. time : 15 mins.** ≫ **Cooking time : 15 mins.** ≫ **Makes 6 parathas.**

½ cup paneer, grated
1 cup whole wheat flour (gehun ka atta)
1 to 2 green chillies, finely chopped
2 tablespoons chopped coriander
½ teaspoon roasted cumin seed (jeera) powder
salt to taste

≫ **For layering**
1 tablespoon ghee
1 teaspoon whole wheat flour (gehun ka atta)

≫ **Other ingredients**
ghee for serving

1. Combine all the ingredients together and crumble the paneer into the flour till the mixture resembles bread crumbs.
2. Knead into a soft and pliable dough, adding water as required.
3. Keep the dough aside for 10 to 15 minutes.
4. Divide the dough into 4 equal parts.
5. Roll out one portion to a 150 mm. (6") diameter circle and evenly spread a little melted ghee on the surface.
6. Sprinkle a little flour and pleat the dough lengthwise into 1 collected strip.
7. Twist this strip and coil into a circle.
8. Flatten this coil and roll into a circle of about 200 mm. (8") diameter.
9. Moisten the lower half of this paratha with some water and place this side on a hot tava.
10. When the paratha starts to speckle a little, reverse the tava gently and allow the other side of the paratha to cook over the open flame.
11. Cook till both sides are browned and crispy and peel the paratha off the tava.
Serve hot smeared with some ghee.

Khasta Roti

The term khasta denotes a crumbly texture. This is one of my favourite rotis and makes an excellent accompaniment to Mutter Paneer Butter Masala, page.....

಄ **Prep. time : 10 mins.** ಄ **Cooking time : 15 mins.** ಄ **Makes 4 rotis.**

¾ cup whole wheat flour (gehun ka atta)
¼ cup semolina (rawa)
3 tablespoons ghee
salt to taste

1. Combine all the ingredients together using your fingertips to get a crumbly mixture.
2. Add enough water to make a semi soft dough. Take care not to knead the dough too much as it will lose its crumbly texture.
3. Cover the dough with a damp muslin cloth and keep aside for 10 to 15 minutes.
4. Divide the dough into 4 equal portions and roll out each portion, using a little wheat flour, to a circle of 100 mm. (4") diameter.
5. Moisten one surface with a little water and place the roti, with the moistened surface facing down on a hot iron griddle (tava) with a handle.
6. Cook over a medium flame for 2 to 3 minutes, then turn the pan over (the roti should be stuck to the pan) and roast the other a side over direct flame till it gets golden spots.
7. Place the pan back over the flame and roast the moistened side of the roti till it is golden in color.
8. Repeat to make 3 more rotis. Serve immediately.

Ajwaini Roti

A simple whole wheat roti spiked up with the delicate flavours of ajwain. Serve them with a simple vegetable dish and some pickle to make a satisfying working lunch.

❧ **Prep. time : 10 mins.** ❧ **Cooking time : 10 mins.** ❧ **Makes 4 rotis.**

1 cup whole wheat flour (gehun ka atta)
½ teaspoon ajwain (carom seeds)
2 teaspoon oil
salt to taste

❧ **Other ingredients**
ghee for cooking

1. Combine all the ingredients and mix well.
2. Add enough water and knead to a soft dough. Keep covered for 10 to 15 minutes.
3. Divide the dough into 4 equal portions.
4. Roll out each portion into a round of 100 mm. (4") diameter.
5. Roast the roti on either side, using a little ghee, on a hot tava, till both sides are golden brown.

Serve immediately.

Kashmiri Roti

Like all other Kashmiri preparations, this roti has a delicate blend of spices.
I have used milk to bind the dough instead of water as this helps to enrich the roti. You may even add saffron if you desire.

෨ **Prep. time : 10 mins.** ෨ **Cooking time : 20 mins.** ෨ **Makes 3 rotis.**

1 cup whole wheat flour (gehun ka atta)
¼ teaspoon cumin seeds (jeera)
¼ teaspoon fennel seeds (saunf)
½ teaspoon pepper, crushed
a pinch asafoetida (hing)
¼ teaspoon ajwain (carom seeds)
¾ cup warm milk
salt to taste

෨ **Other ingredients**
ghee for cooking

1. Mix all the ingredients together and knead into a semi soft dough. Keep covered with a damp muslin cloth for 10 to 15 minutes.
2. Divide the dough into 3 equal portions and roll out each portion into 6 mm . (¼") thickness rounds.
3. Cook on a hot griddle (tava) over a low flame, using ghee, till both the sides are golden brown in colour.

Serve hot.

Phulkas / Chapatis

Picture on facing page

Chapatis or phulkas is the daily bread for millions of Indians. No meal is complete without them and yet many find them difficult to make. These are called so because they swell up with steam while being cooked. They are cooked first on a dry hot tava, then held directly over a flame where they "phulao" ("swell" in Hindi) with steam to the point of bursting. Serve them hot with a dollop of ghee.

Prep. time : 10 mins. Cooking time : 15 mins. Makes 6 phulkas.

1 cup whole wheat flour (gehun ka atta)
½ teaspoon salt
1 teaspoon oil

Other ingredients
ghee for serving

1. Combine the flour and salt and knead into a soft and pliable dough.
2. Add the oil and knead again till it is smooth and elastic.
3. Cover and keep aside for 10 to 15 minutes.
4. Divide the dough into 6 equal parts.
5. Roll out each one using a little flour into approx. 150 mm. (6") diameter circles. Dust dry flour as required to facilitate even rolling.
6. Dust off any excess dry flour and place the chapati on a hot tava.
7. Turn over in a few seconds and cook this side till the edges begin to curl slightly and small blisters appear on the surface.
8. Cook the other side for a few more seconds.
9. Lift the chapati with a pair of flat tongs and roast on both sides over an open flame till it puffs up.
10. Flatten the chapati and apply some ghee on top.
11. Repeat to make 5 more chapatis.
Serve hot.

Top: Vaal Drumsticks, page 96
Bottom: Phulkas/Chapatis, recipe above

Makai Methi Roti

The methi used in combination with makai ka atta makes a delectable variation of the traditional makai ki roti.
A bowl of thick curds is all that is required along with these rotis to make a satisfying breakfast or a quick meal.

Prep. time : 10 mins. ☞ Cooking time : 10 mins. ☞ Makes 4 rotis.

1 cup maize flour (makkai ka atta)
¼ cup fenugreek (methi) leaves, chopped
1 green chilli, chopped
2 teaspoons oil
salt to taste

☞ To serve
2 teaspoons butter

1. Mix all the ingredients together and using enough water, knead to make a soft dough.
2. Divide the dough into 4 equal portions.
3. Roll out each portion into 125 mm. (5") diameter circles.
4. Cook on a hot tava till both sides are golden brown.
Serve hot with a dollop of butter.

Puris

Picture on page 49

These light and fluffy "pillows" are ubiquitous with heavy holiday or festive meals.
Makes them spicy by adding some spices by adding some spices to the dough and you won't even need a vegetable dish to serve them with.

Prep. time : 15 mins. Cooking time : 15 mins. Makes 10 puris.

1 cup whole wheat flour (gehun ka atta)
1 tablespoon semolina (rava)
2 tablespoons oil
salt to taste

Other ingredients
oil for deep frying

1. Combine all the ingredients and knead into a firm dough using water.
2. Knead well and keep aside for 10 to 15 minutes.
3. Divide the dough into 10 equal portions and roll out each portion into a 75 mm. (3") diameter round.
4. Deep fry in oil on both sides till golden brown.
5. Drain on absorbent paper and serve hot.

Lachcha Parathas

Picture on page 21

A crispy paratha, with many, many layers which gives it the name "lachcha"

Prep. time : 20 mins. **Cooking time : 20 mins.** **Makes 8 parathas.**

2 cups whole wheat flour (gehun ka atta)
1 teaspoon salt
3 tablespoons oil
warm water for kneading

Other Ingredients
ghee for cooking

1. Sieve the flour and salt together in bowl. Rub in the oil and add warm water gradually. Knead until smooth.
2. Cover and leave aside for 20 minutes.
3. Knead again and divide the dough into 8 portions. Shape each into a round ball. Flatten a little.
4. Roll out each flattened ball into a 150 mm. (6") diameter circle. Cut into 50 mm. (2") strips lengthways. Place all the strips over the center one.
5. Roll like a Swiss roll. Press a little with your fingers. Pour 1 teaspoon of oil on each roll.
6. Take one roll at a time and roll it out into a round of about 125 mm. (5") diameter.
7. When you remove the round, place it on your palms and lightly press towards the center to show the layers clearly.
8. Heat a tava and cook the rounds lightly on both sides. When you want to serve, cook the rounds directly on the gas or preferably on charcoal. Apply ghee and serve hot.

Bajra Aloo Roti

Picture on page 59

Prep. time : 5 mins. **Cooking time : 10 mins.** **Makes 6.**

2 cups bajra flour (black millet flour)
¾ cup potatoes, boiled and mashed
½ teaspoon crushed pepper
salt to taste

Other ingredients
ghee for cooking

1. Combine all the ingredients to make a soft dough, using warm water.
2. Divide the dough into 6 equal portions and roll out each portion into a 150 mm. (6") diameter circle.
3. Cook the rotis on a hot tava (griddle) using a little ghee, until both sides are golden brown.

Serve hot.

VADE

Picture on cover page

Vade are traditional Maharashtrian version of the deep fried puris. The authentic recipe calls for a lot of pre-preparation in terms of making the flour for the vadas at home. I have used the readymade rice flour for a quick and delicious version.

Prep. time : 5 mins. Cooking time : 10 mins. Makes 6 vades.

2 cups rice flour (chawal ka atta)
1 cup whole wheat flour (gehun ka atta)
salt to taste

Other ingredients
oil for deep frying

1. Mix together all the ingredients and using enough hot water knead into a soft dough.
2. Cover and keep aside for 15 to 20 minutes.
3. Divide the dough into 6 equal portions and roll out each portion, on a greased sheet of plastic, into a 50 mm. (2") diameter round.
4. Deep fry in hot oil until golden brown in colour.
Serve immediately.

Best sellers by
Tarla Dalal

INDIAN COOKING

Rotis & Subzis

Desi Khana

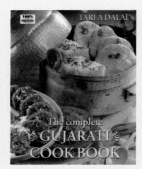

The Complete
Gujarati Cook Book

Rajasthani Cook Book

Chaat

Achaar aur Parathe

Tava Cooking

Cooking with
1 Teaspoon of Oil

Dessert Collection

Ice-Creams
& Frozen Desserts

Mithai

Eggless Desserts

The Chocolate
Cook Book